"The great tide of Emigration flows steadily westward. The principal emigrants are Irish peasants and laborers. It is calculated that at least four of every five persons who leave the shores of the old country to try their fortunes in the new, are Irish. Since the fatal days of the potato famine and the cholera, the annual numbers of emigrants have gone on increasing, until they have become so great as to suggest the idea, and almost justify the belief, of a gradual depopulation of Ireland."

The Illustrated London News, 6 July 1850

CONTENTS

THE IRISH FAMINE

Peter Gray

DISCOVERIES

HARRY N. ABRAMS, INC., PUBLISHERS

Travelers in early-19th-century Ireland were struck by the island's poverty. To many, the condition of the "peasantry" appeared uniquely primitive. Various explanations for Irish privation were put forward: Some blamed religious error or political agitation, others an excessive birth rate or a lack of individual enterprise. More sympathetic observers pointed to oppressive landlords and British "misgovernment."

CHAPTER I

A NATION OF PAUPERS? IRELAND BEFORE 1845

"Misery, naked, and famishing, that misery which is vagrant, idle, and mendicant, covers the entire country…it follows you everywhere, and besieges you incessantly…and if the voice does not excite profound pity, it importunes and terrifies you."
    Gustave de Beaumont
    Ireland: Social, Political, and Religious, 1839

While contemporary perceptions were shaped by the cultural bias of individual observers, they contained a core of truth. Ireland was indeed a poor society in European terms. Although there was nothing inevitable about the Great Famine of 1845–50, it would not have been possible without the existence of

Ireland was predominantly Catholic and England predominantly Protestant. An Irish rebellion against Protestant control in the 1640s was brutally suppressed by the Puritanical English statesman Oliver Cromwell (left), who offered Catholic landowners the choice of "hell or Connacht."

three interrelated problems: widespread poverty, over-population, and excessive dependence on the potato.

A Colonial Legacy

Ireland was partially colonized by England in the 12th century. A long series of wars, rebel-lions, and confiscations followed the expansion of English rule in the 16th and 17th centuries, disrupting the develop-ment of Irish society. Whole regions were devastated and denuded of people, then repopulated with varying success by

English, Welsh, and Scottish settlers. It was not until late in the 17th century that the population began to recover, reaching about two million by 1700. The replacement of Catholic landowners by their Protestant conquerors led to deeply ingrained distrust and hostility.

Colonialism brought certain benefits in its wake, such as more modern agricultural methods and new crops (including the potato), but the brutality of the conquest left a poisonous legacy. The agricultural innovations made by new landowners, aimed primarily at increasing production of cash crops and livestock for export, were often resented by the tenantry. The Gaelic (Irish-language) tradition in literature and popular culture kept

Catholic hopes were dashed by the victory of the Protestant William III over the Catholic James II at the battle of the Boyne in 1690. Many of James' exiled followers joined continental armies. By the early 18th century, only fourteen percent of Irish land was owned by Catholics, who made up over three-quarters of the population.

Ireland's geography helped shape its history. The mild, damp climate influenced by the Atlantic Gulf Stream was better suited to cattle and sheep grazing than to crop cultivation, at least before the adaptable potato was introduced in the 17th century. In a country intersected by mountain ranges and extensive bogs, internal communication was difficult and regional differences pronounced: The good soil and drier climate of the east and midlands (Leinster) contrasted with the mountainous and boggy west (Connacht, parts of the southern province of Munster, and the northern province of Ulster). Coal and industrial minerals were rare. Most importantly, Ireland's proximity to the larger and wealthier island of Great Britain ensured that population movements and political conflict with its neighbor would be endemic. British interest in Ireland was stimulated by the availability of land, and the risks that an independent Ireland might pose to national security.

alive a deep animosity under the mostly calm surface of 18th-century Ireland, linking the dispossession of the Catholic elite to the grievances of the lower classes.

A series of penal laws were introduced by Britain after 1691 in an attempt to break the Catholic spirit and induce conversion. These laws, which denied political and economic rights to Catholics, had only limited success: The Church survived persecution and the laity adopted strategies to minimize the economic consequences of the laws. Yet their existence reminded Catholics of their inferior status and of the alien nature of their landlords.

The Famine of 1741

Eighteenth-century Ireland witnessed extremes of prosperity and distress. The years of growth following 1690 were followed by grain failures in the late 1720s, which pushed the poor into an ever-greater dependence on potatoes. The bad seasons culminated in 1739–41, when the potato also failed. This led to the worst demographic disaster before 1845: Up to a quarter of a million people died out of a population of about 2,400,000. In popular tradition 1741 was recalled as *Bliadhain an áir* (the Year of the Slaughter), but it has subsequently been almost forgotten. Contemporaries regarded famine as outside the sphere of political responsibility, and it was only in the late 18th century that famine relief came to be seen as a state obligation. Moreover, 1741 was followed by a long period of economic development and demographic expansion.

The Tillage Revolution

In the 1750s the Irish agricultural economy began to grow rapidly with the rise of the trans-Atlantic food trade. Dairying and pig raising replaced cattle and sheep grazing. The population began to increase in a sustained way, partially in response to a greater demand for labor. In the 1770s this growth was accelerated by the beginnings of a rapid expansion of tillage (crop cultivation). As England's population grew and that country became a grain importer, rising corn prices created incentives for greater Irish production. As more land was given over to grain, the use of potatoes also increased. The root was vital in breaking up land for sowing and in providing food for cottiers (farmworkers who rented small plots of land).

The Napoleonic Wars of 1792–1815 further stimulated tillage expansion by boosting prices and profits for farmers and landowners. Cultivation was pushed westward from the drier and more fertile east and on

Migrant farmworkers (*spailpíní*)—pictured below at a job fair with their light spades or "loys"—were able to find enough harvest work in the arable lowlands to support their small farms on the poor soil of the west. Income from the sale of pigs and from the illegal distillation of *poitín* (whiskey) also helped these small-landholders or "cottiers" to pay their rents. Most of the rural poor lived in clustered "clachan" settlements, and many held their land

under the "rundale" or joint-tenancy system, whereby small plots were intermingled and reallocated at intervals. Few laborers were without some land, and cooperation within extended families and communities was common.

to higher ground. Labor, not machinery, was the main input, and access to land rather than wages became the chief mode of payment.

Cottiers' cabins in a "clachan" settlement in County Kerry (left). Cabins were built with local stones or turf and thatched with rush or straw. Most were without windows and had only a hole in the roof to let smoke escape. Pigs, poultry, and other animals shared the interior with the family.

Ascendancy and Rebellion

In the 1760s the increasingly wealthy Anglo-Irish elite adopted a more confrontational attitude towards its British rulers. Constitutional reforms were won between 1779 and 1783, but the Anglo-Irish were unable to maintain them against the determined British Prime Minister, William Pitt. Even so, the Irish Parliament's obstruction of Pitt's policies convinced him that full political union was desirable.

Three strands combined to create an explosive situation in the 1790s. First, United Irish radicals called for parliamentary reform and, when this was rejected, for separation from Britain. Second, Catholics became increasingly assertive in demanding readmission to political life and were encouraged by the American and French revolutions. Pitt conceded the vote to certain Catholic tenants in 1793, but was prevented from granting more by a "Protestant ascendancy" backlash. Third, population pressure and political excitement in religiously mixed south Ulster produced sectarian conflict. The rival societies that emerged—Protestant Orangemen and

The growing wealth of 18th-century Ireland was reflected in Georgian "big houses" (below). Anglo-Irish landowners intended such edifices to represent their permanence in Ireland and their political and social prestige.

Catholic Defenders—were incorporated into opposing sides: the government and the United Irishmen.

In 1794 the United Irishmen became an underground conspiracy, allied with France. Their failed uprising of 1798 had long-lasting consequences: Radical leaders were executed or exiled, bequeathing a romantic revolutionary tradition to Irish political culture. Exaggerated reports of sectarian massacres during the uprising stoked renewed anti-Catholic feeling. Tension between Protestant landlords and Catholic tenants in the affected areas also endured.

The Irish Parliament (above) embodied Protestant pride and identity in the 18th century. "Patriots" criticized the mercantilist policies that had subordinated Ireland within the British empire and, supported by the armed "Volunteers," extracted trade concessions in 1779 and legislative autonomy in 1782. Presbyterians and Catholics remained dissatisfied and demanded more radical change. Inspired by the American and French revolutions, many joined the United Irishmen in 1791. In 1792 crowds marched through Belfast to commemorate the fall of the Bastille and demand liberty for Ireland (left).

ANNO TRICESIMO NONO & QUADRAGESIMO

GEORGII III. REGIS.

✱✱✱

C A P. LXVII.

An Act for the Union of *Great Britain* and *Ireland*.
[2d *July* 1800.]

WHEREAS in purfuance of His Majefty's moft gracious Re- Preaml
commendation to the Two Houfes of Parliament in *Great
Britain* and *Ireland* refpectively, to confider of fuch Meafures
as might beft tend to ftrengthen and confolidate the Connection between
the Two Kingdoms, the Two Houfes of the Parliament of *Great Britain*
and the Two Houfes of the Parliament of *Ireland* have feverally agreed
and refolved, that, in order to promote and fecure the effential Interefts
of *Great Britain* and *Ireland*, and to confolidate the Strength, Power,
and Refources of the *Britifh* Empire, it will be advifeable to concur in
fuch Meafures as may beft tend to unite the Two Kingdoms of *Great
Britain* and *Ireland* into One Kingdom, in fuch Manner, and on fuch
Terms and Conditions, as may be eftablifhed by the Acts of the refpective
Parliaments of *Great Britain* and *Ireland*:

The Union

The 1800 Act of Union merged the Irish Parliament with
that of Great Britain. Pitt's promise that the Union would
be followed by speedy emancipation—the admission of
Catholics to parliament and official positions—was not
kept because of the staunch opposition of the king and
British opinion. Petitions from moderate Catholics were
rejected and tensions rose as the Dublin administration
allied itself with the Protestant Orange Order.

This situation was exploited by the radical lawyer
Daniel O'Connell, who revived the emancipation
campaign in 1823. His Catholic Association mobilized

William Pitt took
advantage of the
1798 revolt to introduce a
Union bill, but he found
persuading the Dublin
Parliament to vote itself
out of existence more
difficult than he had
anticipated. The govern-
ment had to convince the
commercial world of its
benefits, to assure the
Catholic clergy that
emancipation would
follow, and to
compensate Protestant
owners of political
"property" (such as seats
and offices), before the
bill could be passed. Lord
Castlereagh, the Irish
Secretary, described this
bargaining as "buying out
the fee-simple [full
property right] of Irish
corruption." Opponents
condemned such bribery
as immoral and argued
that the Union was
illegitimate. Any hopes
that a united parliament
would be more liberal
were soon dashed. The
act abolished the separate
Irish Parliament and
gave Ireland one hundred
seats in the House
of Commons in
Westminster, but
left intact the Irish
administration at Dublin
Castle, headed by a Lord
Lieutenant (usually a
nobleman) and a Chief
Secretary. Both were
usually English and
appointed from London.

large numbers who participated at public meetings and paid a monthly "Catholic rent." O'Connell hoped to wean the rural poor away from agrarian conspiracies and to incorporate them into a national political movement. Always careful to stay within the letter of the law and to keep the sympathy of British and Irish liberals, he began campaigns that culminated in electoral revolts by the Catholic tenantry in 1826–8. Faced with a political crisis in Ireland, the government gave way and introduced an emancipation bill in 1829.

While the emancipation bill addressed the "Catholic question," it failed to resolve it, and many of the poor expressed disillusionment in the aftermath of the bill. Recognizing this, O'Connell adopted a strategy that oscillated between seeking popular reforms by parliamentary means and returning to mass agitation. In the early 1830s he took up the cry to repeal the Union, demanding Irish self-government within the empire. O'Connell was prepared to put such campaigning aside when a Whig-liberal government offered pro-Catholic reforms between 1835 and 1841, but with the return to power of Robert Peel's Conservatives, such conciliation appeared hopeless, and the Repeal campaign was revived.

An inspired orator, whose family came from the Gaelic gentry, Daniel O'Connell (above) had, by 1808, pushed the moderates out of the Catholic movement. His aim was to use mass grievances over Protestant political, religious, and social privileges to build a democratic and liberal nationalist movement.

Peel's government briefly imprisoned O'Connell in 1844 and proposed reforms to woo the Catholic clergy and middle classes: The Catholic seminary at Maynooth received an augmented grant, and three university colleges open to Catholics were established. Peel also initiated an inquiry into the land system, although he had no intention of conceding popular demands for lower rents or "fixity of tenure."

O'Connell may not have been overly dismayed at the suppression of agitation; the strength of Irish popular feeling had been expressed, and by 1845 he was prepared to return to a pact with the Whigs, with land reform as the central platform. Although some romantic nationalists were impatient for "action," O'Connell was convinced that every reform would ultimately strengthen the case for self-government.

In 1843 O'Connell attracted crowds of over 100,000 to more than thirty "monster meetings," such as the one at the ancient site of Tara (opposite below) and in Dublin (below). He combined an all-embracing call to repeal the Union with local grievances to create a powerful force for change. These political

The Pre-Famine Economy

Nationalists blamed the Union for economic decline in the early 19th century. The Union brought free trade between Britain and Ireland and began the process of integrating their economic institutions. By the 1820s the duties that had protected Irish manufactures had disappeared. Yet it is difficult to say whether an Irish parliament could have done much to alleviate the

spectacles and the popular press spread nationalist consciousness in the countryside. For many of the rural poor, attendance at such meetings was also a declaration of defiance to their landlords.

economic dislocations of the period, such was the economic power and proximity of industrializing Britain. Only Belfast (in the north) and its hinterland made a successful transition to factory production and shared many interests with Britain. In general, opening the economy to international markets further exposed a weakened Ireland to potential disaster.

The real downturn in the economy began around 1815. The boom years of the Napoleonic Wars came to an end, leaving Ireland to face an agricultural crisis. Poor harvests brought famine conditions to some areas in 1816–7 and 1822. Prices fell and monetary deflation from 1819 made landlords' debts more burdensome. Yet for farmers the postwar years were not all gloomy; prices recovered in the 1830s, and there is evidence that some saw growing prosperity.

Rigorous Methods of Estate Management

In the 18th century many proprietors, especially "absentees"—those not actually living on their property—had been happy to rent their

Exports of grain and livestock continued to grow in response to rising British demand, and Irish farmers received some benefit from the Corn Laws, which restricted foreign grain imports in 1815. Higher livestock prices and the arrival of quick steamship transport across the Irish Sea in the 1820s encouraged landowners and large farmers to consider returning their land to grazing, but widespread resistance from laborers and smallholders—who faced eviction to make way for animals—restricted this develop-ment before 1845. Below: The bustling marketplace of Ennis, County Clare, in the 1820s.

land on very long leases to "middlemen" tenants in return for a steady rent. It was understood that these middlemen would sublet to under-tenants to maximize their agricultural income. Many middlemen were in fact the descendants of dispossessed Catholic landowners and were retained because they could guarantee some social stability. This class of former landowners was regarded as useful until rapidly rising prices left the fixed rents paid to landlords lagging in the late 18th century. After 1815 most landowners moved to take personal control and as leases expired, middlemen were removed. Landlords gave their smaller tenants only yearly "tenancies-at-will," which made eviction easier.

Dublin (above) suffered from absentee landlords and industrial stagnation after the Union, but the city remained a major produce exporter.

Influenced by British practices, proprietors wanted to overhaul farming methods and introduce large farms worked by landless laborers. Landlords had little sympathy and felt no moral responsibility for the large numbers of smallholders and cottiers who remained on their estates.

The Linen Trade

The rise of domestic industry in the Irish countryside added further momentum to population growth. Irish linen exports had risen by a factor of eighty in the 18th century, making it the most valuable export commodity. Linen production was widespread in the northern part of Ireland by the 1780s. Weaving and spinning involved entire rural families; the finished goods were bought by merchants who sold them in the great linen markets of Belfast and Dublin.

Handloom weavers did not abandon agriculture, but divided their energies between industrial output and subsistence cultivation on small plots. The high rents

Despite the grinding poverty, pre-Famine Ireland was renowned for the exuberance of its folk tradition in music and dance. "Recreational" fighting among members of opposing political factions was also widespread until the 1830s.

made possible by this system encouraged landlords and middlemen to allow subdivision, facilitating early marriages and large families. By 1800 Armagh, the center of the linen trade, was the most densely populated county in Ireland, and large linen-dependent populations had arisen on poor land in Mayo, Sligo, Leitrim, and Roscommon.

However, by the 1820s the domestic industrial sector was severely reduced. This contraction was part of the concentration of manufacturing in Britain that followed technological advance. By 1826 the cotton industry in Ireland had collapsed. Belfast was able to weather this crisis by switching its factories to linen spinning, using new techniques in which the city increasingly specialized.

As linen production was mechanized, the extensive network of domestic laborers became redundant in north Connacht, south Ulster, and north Leinster. Many families were forced to survive off their tiny potato patches and faced an acute collapse in living standards. The woolen industry in Munster suffered a similar fate. The roots of the Great Famine lay as much in industrial as in agricultural malaise in these areas.

Agrarian Secret Societies

The scale of change in late-18th-century Ireland inevitably produced social tensions. A series of disturbances in the 1760s, known collectively as "Whiteboyism," but with different names in various localities, alarmed the propertied classes. These movements were concerned more with upholding a rural "moral economy" and keeping down taxes and

"Throughout the greater part of Ulster, land is held in very small portions; and the superior comforts of the country people have been, in some considerable degree, owing to the domestic linen manufacture."
Henry Inglis
A Journey throughout Ireland, 1835

The British government usually responded to disturbances with new legislation and armed police: The Irish Constabulary (below) was established as a national force in 1836.

rents than with dispossessing landowners.

Agrarian disturbances were organized by secret societies. Most of their activity was localized and apolitical, although some political elements survived from the uprising of 1798 among the Ribbon Societies in the northern part of the island. Agrarian movements were often directed at grievances within the rural population, which observers called the "peasantry." Landless laborers or land-poor cottiers (holding less than five acres and partially dependent on working for others) often combined to force farmers to employ local men, to keep up wages, or to ensure continuing access to cheap "conacre" plots of less than an acre.

At other times broader "peasant" coalitions could be formed against such common targets as landlords, middlemen, and large livestock-grazing farmers. This was especially the case in the 1820s as rents rose and a movement towards consolidation of land began. Tipperary, a fertile and densely populated county, became notorious as the hotbed of agrarian societies ready to intimidate, injure, and murder those landlords, agents, and poor "land-grabbers" who dared to infringe upon the unwritten agrarian code. Such agrarian "outrages" and the tacit support they received from local communities terrified and angered landowners.

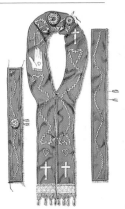

Contemporaries regarded agrarian societies as "a vast trade union for the protection of the Irish peasantry." Secrecy and ritual were essential elements of the movement. Above: The green sash of a Ribbon lodge. Below: "Rockites" swearing in a new member to their agrarian society in the 1820s.

Population and Poverty

Population continued to rise, from around five million in 1800 to seven million in 1821 and eight and a half million in 1845. Yet the momentum slowed markedly after 1821 in response to the changed economic climate. During the period 1830–45 the rate of growth was below the European average. While this fall can partly be attributed to growing emigration, prudential restraint also played a role, especially for farmers, who had begun to marry later. However, these trends varied geographically and socially.

In the 1840s the population of Ireland reached a plateau. The average density on cultivated land was about 700 people per square mile, among the highest in Europe. The very poor had increased as a proportion of the population, and few alternative occupations were available outside the overstaffed agricultural sector.

The writings of the English economist Thomas Malthus concentrated attention on the relationship between population and poverty from 1798 on. His pessimistic teachings were applied to the Irish case, especially when famine brought the matter to public attention in 1817 and 1822. However, by the 1830s many English observers had come to see Ireland's problem less as an excess of population than as a lack of capital investment.

On the better lands, "comfortable" farmers (renting over fifteen acres) coexisted with "cottiers"—who held about five acres and required paid work to supplement their incomes—and with laborers—who rented manured "conacre" plots of less than an acre to grow a single crop of potatoes. Extortionate sums were frequently demanded for "conacre," and it was a source of constant tension. As the economy contracted after 1815, many farmers were forced into begging or poaching to live. Others, particularly in the north-west, became seasonal migrant laborers in the fields of Scotland and England or joined the gangs building canals and railroad lines.

A Poor Law for Ireland

For the government, alleviating Irish poverty meant stimulating economic development. In 1831 the state took responsibility for elementary education and for "public works" such as roadbuilding and inland navigation. Government officials were, however, eager that Irish landowners met their share of the burden and rejected an 1836 report proposing a massive works and assisted-emigration program. Instead, they introduced a poor law modeled on the new English workhouse system. This was supported by the Catholic clergy as a fair act for the poor and by officials as a means of loosening the poor's attachment to the land.

While the state in Ireland was among the most interventionist in Europe, it failed to undertake the massive structural changes that might have transformed the country. This lack of action was caused partly by a failure of vision, by the restraints imposed by the ideology of laissez-faire (letting things take their course), and by vested interests and party antagonisms.

In 1845 Ireland's highly commercialized export sector existed alongside an impoverished subsistence economy, the product of unrestricted capitalist development. Internal adjustment was painfully slow, and in the meantime the country was highly vulnerable to such an unforeseen event as the potato blight.

The general decrease in population was not noted in the "clachan" communities of the west coast, which continued to expand, reclaiming barren land for potato cultivation and fertilizing the fields with seaweed. Low material expectations and the fecundity of the potato account for this continuing growth, but landowners in these remote districts welcomed such development, because it generated some rent despite minimal investment. Small-scale fishing was also practiced in the west, but fish remained a luxury, and potatoes were the subsistence food of fishermen. Below: Burning seaweed for kelp, used to make soap and glass, in Connemara— a declining occupation by the 1830s.

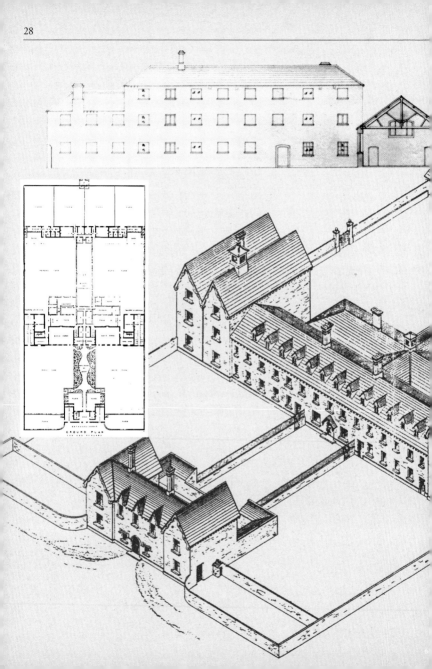

GROUND PLAN

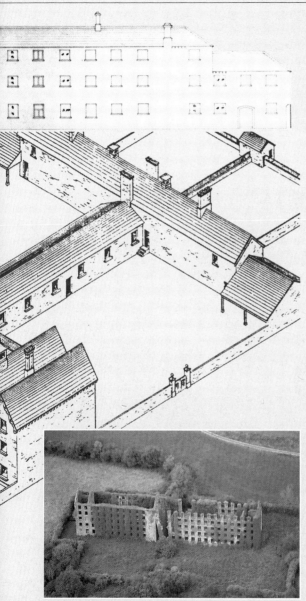

Under the 1838 poor law, Ireland was divided into 130 poor-law unions, each containing a workhouse. Boards of Guardians, elected by local taxpayers and responsible to a resident commissioner in Dublin, regulated each union. The workhouses were designed to house some 100,000 destitute people, well short of the 2,400,000 the royal commission had declared in 1836 to be in a state of "poverty." The act aimed to discourage "pauperism" by enforcing a harsh regime of work, diet, and segregation by age and sex. Hated by the poor, the workhouses were rarely half full before 1845. It was mostly the elderly and ill, and those forced into temporary destitution when potato supplies ran out before the harvest, who resorted to the workhouse. However, the poor law was not designed to cope with famine. When isolated western areas suffered bad harvests in 1842, ad hoc relief works and assistance to local committees were again adopted. Far left: The original plans for Irish workhouses, with separate yards for men, women, and children. Near left: A former mill used as an auxiliary workhouse after 1847.

In 1845 Ireland was extraordinarily dependent on a single subsistence crop—the potato. Out of a population of eight and a half million, over a million and a half landless laborers and their families had no other significant source of food. Three million more, from smallholding and cottier families, were also very largely dependent on the crop. Even the wealthier Irish consumed considerably more potatoes than the British, but it was the rural poor who were most at risk if the crop failed.

CHAPTER II
THE COMING OF THE BLIGHT, 1845–6

"Ireland is threatened with a thing that is read of in history and in distant countries, but scarcely in our own land and time—a famine. Whole fields of the root have rotted in the ground, and many a family sees its sole provision for the year destroyed."

The Spectator
25 October 1845

Mountains, bogs, and turbulent seas isolated much of the western seaboard from the rest of Ireland. In many such places there was little commercial activity despite the soaring population.

Some regions were better suited to meet such an eventuality. In the "oatmeal zones" of Ulster and north Leinster, income from domestic industry still allowed the poor to supplement their diet with oats. In the south and west, however, oats were not available except as a "famine" food. Here too, inferior varieties of potato had become widespread. The prolific but less nutritious "lumper" had made considerable inroads, and varieties that lasted better through the "hungry months" of the summer had ceased to be as widely available.

Consumption of Potatoes Was Extraordinary by Modern Standards

Adult male laborers would eat up to fourteen pounds of potatoes daily, with women and children over ten consuming about eleven pounds and younger children around five pounds. These would be eaten in three equal meals, with a seasoning of salt, cabbage, or fish when available. A meal would be missed if there was a shortage of food or fuel. An estimated seven million tons of potatoes were required each year for human consumption by the 1840s.

The potato-fed Irish remained relatively better nourished and more healthy than the masses in other European countries. Though reviled by British commentators, who treated bread as a "superior" food, the potato provided a well-balanced diet when combined with some dairy and vegetable produce or fish. Below: A potato market in County Waterford in the 1820s.

How much risk did Irish dependence on the potato pose in 1845? With the benefit of hindsight, post-Famine commentators condemned Irish overreliance and pointed to a series of warning signs. These were, however, less obvious to pre-Famine cultivators. Potato failures before 1845 were localized, short-lived, and led to relatively small loss of life, partly because the proportion of the crop fed to animals could be reduced if necessary.

Increasing reliance on the potato reduced its earlier advantage as a means of spreading the risk of crop fluctuations, but there was nothing inevitable about the failures of 1845–9. Before the arrival of the blight, the potato had proved a more reliable staple crop in Ireland than any grain. No one in 1845 predicted the catastrophic events of the following five years.

Nothing was wasted by the farmers: Potato skins and any surplus potatoes were fed to the pigs, which were a central part of the rural domestic economy. Pigs were rarely eaten by the poor, but fattened and sold to raise money for rent. Pigs also helped produce the ubiquitous manure heaps outside cabins, which were vital for fertilizing the intensively cultivated fields.

Phytophthora infestans

The potato blight that appeared in 1845 was a new disease. In its wake it left confusion, wild speculation, and panic in every part of Europe that depended heavily on potatoes. The disease produced an ecological catastrophe almost unparalleled in modern history.

The botanical epidemic was first observed on the eastern seaboard of the United States in 1843, spreading rapidly from the New York area to the midwest by 1845. By the early summer of 1845 it had a foothold in Europe —in Flanders. Ireland, southern France, Switzerland, eastern Germany, and southern Scandinavia were affected by mid-October.

Why was the blight able to spread so quickly? One reason was the development of an international potato-seed trade, in response to fears of potato "degeneracy"

Tom Sullivan's cabin, County Kerry (above): "In answer to our inquiries…he replied that the food of himself and family all the year round was potatoes and buttermilk. 'Were the potatoes good?' 'Troth, they were not, bad as could be'; and he proved the assertion by cutting open a number of them taken at random from the heap, and showing us the extent of the disease."
Pictorial Times
January 1846

and earlier diseases. North America renewed its potato stock and imported guano from Peru, the probable source of the fungus. The seed trade also accounts for the blight's trans-Atlantic leap to the Low Countries. Once established in temperate climates, the blight depended mainly on damp conditions for its propagation.

The blight was first reported in Ireland in early September, but there was little concern until the second week in October. One reason for this was the very large area sown that year, and the excellent early potato crop in August. It was the main crop, usually harvested from October to November, that was diseased. As the blight moved west across Ireland, some areas were spared the full impact of the disaster by early frosts. It was in general the more prosperous eastern regions that were most badly hit in 1845, but there was considerable local variation.

In total about one-third of the late crop was lost that season, although the full impact was not obvious until many of the apparently sound potatoes stored in pits after harvesting were found to be rotten when uncovered. The failure of this subsistence crop was the worst the Irish had experienced for a century. It raised the real specter of famine.

Potato blight is the fungal infestation *Phytophthora infestans*, which thrives in mild, damp conditions and reproduces by means of spores carried by wind or water. The fungus attacks first the leaves and the stalk, before penetrating beneath the soil to consume the tuber. In the moist, sunless summer of 1845 it spread extremely rapidly. Those regions affected early in the growing season were worst hit, but while Ireland suffered relatively late, the particular wetness of its climate ensured that losses would still be considerable. Most botanists misdiagnosed the disease, arguing that it was a wet-rot induced by a particularly damp summer. The minority who attributed the blight to a fungus were ignored by the scientific establishment, and an antidote was not discovered until over thirty years later. Left and above: The diseased tuber and stalk of a potato plant.

The Visitation of God

The majority of people in Europe were predominantly religious in the 1840s, and some sought to reconcile such new sciences as geology, botany, and economics to Christian doctrine. Religious enthusiasm and scientific advance

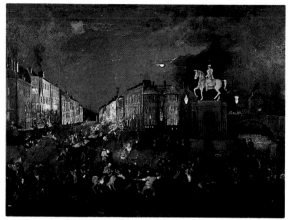

combined to produce an interpretative framework for both natural and social phenomena. It was inevitable that a catastrophe such as the potato blight, bringing with it the Biblical idea of famine, should have been widely described in religious terms.

Many reports spoke of the Irish poor responding with pious fatalism. Their submissive reaction to the natural disaster irritated many observers who complained that the Irish were not trying to save their crops. But in reality there was little that could be done in the face of this unknown and unpredictable disease. If alarm was indeed muted in 1845, it was because Ireland had faced such situations before and had emerged with limited losses. Many British also saw the situation through religious eyes. The "visitation" was widely regarded as a warning against luxury and complacency, but some drew more specific

Some of the poor attributed the blight to "the wrath of God for the sins of the people that's on the land." Sabbath breaking, fighting, and drinking—frequent at such festivals as Skellig night (above, in Cork)—were mentioned as possible reasons for divine anger. The Catholic Church, which had been supporting a temperance campaign since the early 1840s, at first agreed that the disaster pointed to the need for moral reform. Nationalists, meanwhile, saw the crisis as justifying their position; some alleged the blight was the judgment of a "retributive Providence" to punish Irish landlords for abusing their powers.

lessons. Extreme language was common among evangelicals with anti-Catholic leanings, who linked Ireland's plight with its religious "error" and warned that England's toleration of Catholicism would lead to further punishment of such "national sin."

Other observers, probably the majority, refused to believe that divine Providence would inflict such suffering without some compensating mercy. To many the lesson was obvious: Dependence on the potato was "unnatural" and should be replaced with a "higher" diet based on grain. The British radicals of the Anti-Corn Law League, who had long campaigned against food tariffs, took up the cry. Peel had been planning a progressive move to free trade with foreign countries for several years and was aware of both popular expectations and the opportunity raised by the potato failure. Yet he did not act purely from political expediency and privately took a serious view of the workings of divine Providence.

To British millenarian evangelicals expecting the end of the world, the threatened famine in Ireland was a "sign of the times." They anticipated similar evils for England unless it repented. Others believed that God had acted for more specific temporal purposes. The influential London *Times* denounced the potato as the "most precarious of crops and meanest of foods" and declared that divine Providence "evidently intended another subsistence" for Ireland. Irish society was widely regarded as in need of urgent transformation.

Corn, Potatoes, and Maize

Peel's decision to repeal the Corn Laws, which had protected British agriculture from foreign imports through tariffs, threw the country into political crisis. Most of his Conservative party colleagues rejected his proposals and opposed his leadership. Peel was now dependent on the Whig party's support to continue in government, but he clearly believed he had a personal mission.

The tense political situation prompted the relatively rapid and efficient state response to the Irish crisis of 1845–6. Peel could not afford to lose vital political ground by adopting an unpopular relief policy. His political position depended on proving that Ireland really faced imminent famine. The potato failure was investigated by a scientific commission. Its conclusions

Above: All Peel's nightmares— O'Connell, Irish land agitation, the Corn Laws, and British radicals— came to a head with the potato failure.

on the cause of the disease convinced few, and its recommendation that ventilation of the tubers would stop the rot proved false. However, the commission did not underestimate the disease, stating that up to half the crop had been lost. This figure was, in fact, too high, but it bolstered the case for urgent action.

Irish representatives demanded a prohibition on the export of oatmeal from Ireland to England and the immediate opening of the ports to grain imports. The government rejected the former, and political resistance by protectionists delayed the latter. Peel saw a way around this stalemate by the direct purchase of food by the state. In November he authorized the secret purchase of £100,000 worth of Indian corn (maize) from the United States through Baring Brothers. (In the 1840s the British £ was equal to about $4.86.)

These stocks were sufficient to feed about half a million people for three months at a rate of one pound of meal a day. As such they were inadequate for the needs of Ireland during 1845–6, but Peel never intended that the state should feed all the people. Instead, the food held at state depots would be released into the market to regulate the price of provisions and would be made available for purchase at cost price by local relief committees.

Peel's Food Policy and Irish Society

Peel stated to Parliament his wish "to take advantage of this calamity for introducing among the people of Ireland the taste for a better and more certain provision for their support…and thereby diminishing the chances to which they will be constantly liable, of recurrences of this great and mysterious visitation."

This concern for the reordering of Irish social structures and habits is central to the history of the Famine. Relieving suffering was never the sole concern of many politicians. Divisions existed over where the balance should be drawn and over just what changes were desirable and how they should be introduced, but the prevalent belief that famine had been ordained for some providential purpose underlay British thinking.

Sir Robert Peel, who had considerable experience governing Ireland, was convinced that its problems were rooted in social backwardness. He saw maize —cheaply imported from the United States— as a permanent substitute for the potato in the Irish diet, and he intended that the rural poor would become landless laborers, working for wages on the land of substantial farmers. He was confident that Irish agricultural output would rise rapidly if this social reorganization was accompanied by the challenge of free trade and by an increased investment in scientific "high farming." He was certain private corn merchants (opposite) would develop the maize trade once it was freed from taxation.

Relief Measures

Peel's strategy was to cooperate with Irish landowners, whom he hoped would take local responsibility for relief. About 650 local committees, dominated by the gentry, were set up early in 1846. These bodies were expected to supply the poor with affordable food and received state donations equal to the charitable subscriptions they raised. It was recognized that in some isolated areas such committees could not function, and sub-depots were authorized to distribute food to those in extreme want.

A central relief commission in Dublin was formed to oversee the system. Sir Randolph Routh, its eventual chairman and the head of the commissariat department, fully endorsed the official line on the desirability of replacing potatoes with maize, but disagreements arose over other measures. The commission questioned the government's reliance on the goodwill of landowners, and complained that neither their public spirit nor their spending was adequate.

Administrators preferred a compulsory and permanent mechanism, based on the poor law, for dealing with extreme destitution. This suggestion was vetoed by officials. Peel insisted that relief measures remain temporary, that landowners retain considerable freedom of action, and that the state should provide only transitional aid.

The Public Works Began

The government placed the greatest burden on the Board of Works. Confusion existed from the beginning, as it was intended that the Board organize not only permanent improvements such as land drainage and harbor construction, but also a system of relief works designed primarily to give employment and wages to the destitute.

Charles Trevelyan, the most senior civil servant at the Treasury in London, was entrusted with overseeing every significant item of relief spending. His control over Irish policy grew as the Famine continued, and he imposed his own rigid moralistic agenda with ruthless enthusiasm. Trevelyan's main concern from early 1846 was "to teach the people to depend upon themselves for developing the resources of the country, instead of having recourse to the assistance of the Government on every occasion."

In both cases local landowners were expected to take the initiative and contribute to the expense. In practice very few took advantage of loans made available for the first category of works, and a concerted effort was made to oblige the Board to take full responsibility. The government's policy of granting half the cost of road works inadvertently encouraged this attitude, and even when the landlord-dominated "presentment sessions" initiated works themselves, many hoped that these loans would never have to be repaid.

Government officials intended that the British Treasury's control over relief finances would curb any abuse, yet they took upon themselves the power of relaxing the rules if necessary. In practice they also accelerated the distribution of food from the depots and increased the supply of employment on the public works, in response to civil disturbances.

It was inevitable that the relief measures of 1845–6 should have faced considerable criticism in Britain. Much of this was ideologically motivated and drew on stereotypes of Irish peasant indolence and landlord opportunism. Critics used official evidence of abuses to justify their hostility. The most telling objections concerned the choice of those employed on the relief works and whether the jobs were properly distributed.

Peel had Reason for Self-Congratulation in 1846

Despite criticism of the relief measures, very few people actually died of starvation or disease, and reports from the localities contained many expressions of gratitude (although others praised O'Connell for forcing the government's hand). Maize was now widely consumed, and the arrival of American ships with large cargoes in the summer of 1846 was taken to mean that private trade could now be relied upon to supply Ireland's needs.

The ministry fell in late June, defeated on an Irish coercion bill. Again this bill had more to do with Peel's concern for the permanent alteration of Ireland than with the immediate situation; the crime rate declined as employment became widespread.

No.

We, the undersigned, certify that from he best inquiries we have been able to make,

has lost his Stock of Potatoes by the prevalent Disease, and is a proper object for employment on the Roads carried on by the Board of Works.

Dated at _____ this _____ day of _____ 1846.

_____ } Members of Committee.

By Authority—A. Thom, 87, Abbey-street, Dublin

To be given relief work, the poor had to obtain certificates of destitution (above) from local relief committees, which consisted of landowners, farmers with large holdings, clergy, and professionals. Some committees were accused of providing tickets for employment only to the tenants and dependents of their members, or even of selling them. The most needy applicants were frequently excluded in favor of the better-off. The Irish Board of Works was charged with organizing the public projects. A special relief department was set up, and inspectors, engineers, overseers, and pay clerks dispatched to the provinces, but the relief bureaucracy was soon overwhelmed by local demands and stifled by strict Treasury rules.

The First Year of Famine?

There was great uncertainty about the prospects for the 1846 harvest. Government officials tried to discourage potato planting, yet the Lord Lieutenant was realistic enough to recognize that the poor really had little alternative. While maize or "yellow meal" was tolerated by the poor, few found it a palatable dietary alternative. Surprisingly large stocks of potato seed came to light, and the total acreage planted was only one-fifth less than in 1845. Ireland was gambling for the highest stakes, but the experience of previous years suggested it was worth taking the risk.

Was there then a famine in Ireland in 1845–6? There had been a considerable shortfall in food supply, but mass starvation had been averted. Although much of the grain crop of 1845 had been exported—sufficient to feed up to 1,250,000 people in Britain—the deficit was made up by cheaper imports. This process was partially effective and encouraged a greater planting of grain in 1846. Yet everything depended on the next potato harvest.

The amount of food for human consumption was maintained in 1846 by reducing the number of potatoes fed to animals. Pigs became the first casualties, as many of the poor were forced to sell them prematurely to buy grain. Once deprived of the reliable four-legged rent payer, however, the cottier was in a precarious position. Yet few in Ireland believed the blight would return for a second year. Potato seed had been carefully hoarded, and the apparently healthy state of the young plants in the late spring of 1846 encouraged many laborers to demand, and farmers to provide, conacre plots for potato planting.

Few people died from hunger in Ireland in 1845–6. Prompt state action and the traditional charity of rural communities prevented the worst from occurring. Nevertheless, there was severe suffering in the most marginal social groups.

Continental Europe Was the Worst-Affected Area in 1845–6

Parts of France, Germany, and Switzerland suffered privation, but it was in the Low Countries, where over three-quarters of the potato crop was lost in 1845, that the situation was worst. Like the west of Ireland, Flanders had become vulnerable because of its contracting linen industry. The Netherlands was also heavily dependent on potatoes and suffered from general economic stagnation in the 1840s.

Although grain crops were reasonable in 1845, here too the poor's savings were exhausted and their vulnerability was heightened. The blight would ultimately leave tens of thousands dead in Belgium and the Netherlands by 1847.

In parts of Flanders, half the population was described as living "in the Irish fashion, that is to say on potatoes, vinegar, and water." With the failure of over eighty-five percent of the potato crop in 1845 and the destruction of the rye crop in 1846, conditions became acute. The Belgian state spent a considerable amount of money providing public works and food supplies until 1848. In contrast, the Dutch government chose to ignore the famine in the Netherlands, relying solely on free trade and laissez-faire.

The potato failure in the summer of 1846 exceeded the fears of even the most pessimistic in Ireland. Three to four million people were threatened with starvation by a crop failure unprecedented in the history of modern Europe. Only the British state could command resources sufficient to alleviate such a catastrophe, but employing these effectively required the exercise of administrative wisdom and political will.

CHAPTER III
THE GREAT HUNGER, 1846–7

In September 1846 it was estimated that three-quarters of the potato crop had been destroyed. Police inquiries later put the losses at over nine-tenths. On 25 August a relief official at Ardara, County Donegal, wrote in alarm: "Famine is already upon us."

The blight reappeared first where climatic conditions were most favorable: the mild, moist west of Ireland. It spread relentlessly at a rate of fifty miles per week, propelled by the prevailing winds. After Ireland, the Highlands of Scotland were devastated, but a dry summer in southern England and continental Europe spared these areas in 1846.

By early August virtually the entire surface of Ireland had been ravaged. Eyewitnesses described fields of "luxuriant growth" being reduced overnight to a "wide waste of putrefying vegetation." No human action seemed capable of halting the advance of the blight, and everywhere the general response was one of despair and fear.

Above: An anti-landlord cartoon depicts food exports, used to pay for "His Lordship's Champagne & Burgundy," while the poor cry out in hunger.

The Export Question

As a higher than usual quantity of oats was retained for home consumption, Irish grain exports were one-third lower in 1846 than in the early 1840s. They were equivalent in food value to about one million tons of potatoes, but that was less than one-tenth of the amount destroyed by the blight. Even if exports to Britain had been prohibited, Ireland lacked sufficient food resources to stave off famine in 1846–7.

Exports of any food appeared wrong, given the extent of the disaster, but considerable imports partially dampened the effect. More than twice as much food came into Ireland as left it in 1846–7. Imported maize and rice

were cheaper than the grain sent to Britain, and both merchants and landowners insisted that any ban on exports would destroy the confidence required to secure these shipments, while creating a disincentive for farmers to plant for the following year.

There was a fatal flaw to this logic: Imports from America began to arrive in bulk only in the spring of 1847, after the "starvation gap" of the winter, when the exported grain would have kept many thousands alive. Relief officials drew attention to this problem in the autumn of 1846, but were overruled by the Treasury. Rigid adherence to free trade was the legacy of the Corn Law debates; even Peel declared that the time for intervention was past. The new Whig government formed by Lord John Russell assured the clamorous corn merchants that it would avoid interference in the market and refused to regulate food prices.

To Trevelyan, any meddling with the market forces of supply and demand was counterproductive, but in extensive districts of the Irish west, where the retail trade was underdeveloped or nonexistent, many people had no realistic alternative to state supplies.

After an immediate rush to consume any untainted potatoes, food prices rocketed beyond the reach of the poor. Amid the ensuing panic, grain continued to be exported to Britain to pay the landlords' rent. The palpable injustice of removing this food, seemingly from the mouths of the dying, provoked widespread resistance and left great bitterness. Food convoys guarded by military detachments, as pictured below near Clonmel, County Tipperary, became a common sight in 1846 and 1847.

A New Government

Peel's relief measures of 1845–6 had raised expectations about the ability of the state to act, but the situation facing the incoming Whig government was much worse, involving both an absolute deficit of food in Ireland and a general shortage in Europe. It is unlikely that any government could have prevented considerable loss of life in the circumstances, but the decisions made certainly affected the numbers of deaths.

The powerful "moralist" group in the new cabinet was led by Charles Wood and Lord Henry George Grey, who believed in the optimistic economic ideas of the freetraders. To them Ireland was not overpopulated but underdeveloped; it lacked not capital, but the will to create wealth. Government, they believed, should force the Irish into exerting themselves and working for wages and coerce landowners into fulfilling their "moral duty" to provide employment and relieve destitution.

Trevelyan and the Relief Works

In August 1846 the public works were shut down and thousands of workers laid off. The official intention was to encourage harvest work, but for those previously paid in potatoes or patches of potato ground, there was often nothing to which they could return. In the meantime, the government overhauled the public works system

Much was expected of the new Prime Minister, Lord John Russell (above, with his cabinet). Whig leadership had previously been associated with popular reforms in Ireland, and the Lord Lieutenant, Lord Bessborough, was a personal friend of O'Connell. Other leaders, however, had different priorities. Lords Lansdowne, Palmerston, and Clanricarde were Irish landowners intent on upholding the "rights of property" and were drawn to the ideas of political economy. The Chancellor of the Exchequer, Charles Wood, believed that God had intervened to bring about a "social revolution in Ireland," and he strongly supported Trevelyan.

along the lines recommended by Trevelyan. New legislation increased the responsibility of the Board of Works (which was itself directly answerable to the Treasury) and made the total cost of the works repayable by the localities.

These changes were supposedly aimed at ending abuses. Yet Trevelyan's main objective was to use the public works mechanism to compel laborer and landlord alike to submit to what he deemed the will of heaven. He manipulated the Treasury's powers to break what he denounced as a "cancer of dependency" and to make "Irish property support Irish poverty." Moralists did not have things all their own way, as other ministers insisted on softening this harsh doctrine, but the Treasury did its utmost to operate according to such "sound principle."

The English satirical magazine *Punch* depicted famine as a moral issue. In "Union Is Strength" (left), John Bull (England) presents his Irish "brother" not only with food but a spade, to put him "in a way to earn your own living." *Punch* assumed that self-help was the priority and came to blame Irish indolence for the continuing catastrophe. In "Height of Impudence" (above), published two months later in December 1846, John Bull is accosted by an Irishman who has reverted into a violent stereotype, demanding money for a "blunderbuss." Now "Paddy" is given the apelike features increasingly common in hostile images of the Irish.

The Pressure for Employment Soon Began to Mount

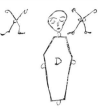

The relief works were restarted in September, but bureaucratic procedures delayed most projects until October. By the end of that month an average of 114,000 were employed daily. This rose to 441,000 by the end of the year. Despite expansion of its staff of engineers, inspectors, and overseers, the Board was overwhelmed. By March 1847 the total cost of the works had reached almost £5 million.

The system fell far short of solving the problems of famine. While food prices spiraled, the wages paid on the works were kept below the "normal" rates of each district. Complaints about the "indolence" of laborers, and a desire to introduce greater "discipline," led to the introduction of a task-work system linking pay to individual exertion. The increasing numbers of malnourished, exhausted, and ill people unable to undertake such strenuous labor found the residual wages of under eight pence (less than forty cents) per day grossly inadequate to feed their starving families.

The Winter Was Harsh and Many, Weakened by Hunger, Were Unable to Buy Turf for Fuel

The Board decided that in bad weather laborers should receive half a day's wages without coming to work, but many of the poor insisted on working rather than see their income sink below what was already starvation level.

In addition to these physical problems, the increasing pointlessness of the works was becoming clear. Any

There was some resistance to the public works regime. Even laborers who were able to benefit from task-work were angered by shortages of tools and lengthy delays in payments. Riots and strikes occurred, and threatening notes (above) were used to intimidate local officials into allowing higher wages. Most relief money was spent on unnecessary "repairs" to existing roads, or on building useless new roads; only small sums were paid out on more beneficial projects such as the railroad viaduct in County Cork (below).

genuine "public" works needed in Ireland had long been completed, but the demand for relief employment seemed insatiable. The Treasury obstructed state spending on works that might benefit any private individual (such as the drainage of land).

For thousands unable to work, the only alternative to the overcrowded and disease-ridden poorhouse was begging in the streets. This woman at Clonakilty, County Cork, asked for only enough money to buy a coffin for her dead child.

By December the failure of the public relief works was indisputable. Reports of mass mortality and inquests attributing deaths to the Board's negligence became common. Thomas Larcom of the relief department reported to London that the system could not be continued. Little of value had been created at a vast expense, labor had been diverted from cultivation, and masses of the rural poor were dying or physically incapacitated. Some new scheme would have to take its place.

Skibbereen

Early in 1847 this small town in County Cork came to be associated with every horror of the Irish Famine. Although by no means unique, it attracted the world's attention. The first death was reported on 24 October. By December the local relief committee had collapsed and people had begun to die in scores.

Food riots again became widespread in 1846–7. With only limited supplies, the government was determined to keep the food depots closed until the last possible moment and then to sell food only at the market price. The crime rate soared as the desperate turned to theft to stay alive. Under famine conditions the prospect of imprisonment or transportation ceased to be a deterrent. In October 1846, two were killed when troops fired on a crowd attacking bakers' shops in Dungarvan, County Waterford (above left). Such collective actions became less frequent in the later years of the Famine.

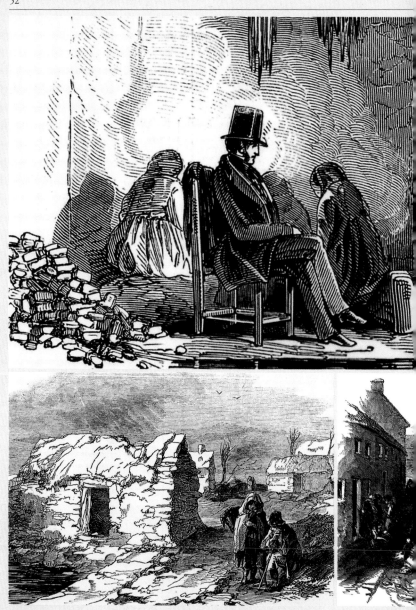

The Irish artist James Mahony visited the Skibbereen area in early 1847. His sketches and notes, published in *The Illustrated London News*, brought the horror of the Famine to the public's notice. Below: "At Cahera…a famished boy and girl turning up the ground to seek for a potato to appease their hunger." Left: The doctor visits a dying man named Mullins at Scull, while his three children seek warmth from the embers of a turf fire. Opposite left: The village of Mienies, where dogs devoured the unburied dead. Below left: "Neither pen nor pencil ever could portray the misery and horror…to be witnessed in Skibbereen …there I saw the dying, the living and the dead, lying indiscriminately upon the same floor, without anything between them and the cold earth, save a few miserable rags upon them."

Private Charity

As the message of Ireland's suffering spread, private charitable work began. The first in the field were the Society of Friends (Quakers), who believed that "when famine stares you in the face, political economy should be forgotten." Philanthropists such as William Forster and James Hack Tuke traveled the stricken west, distributing aid, publicizing their impressions, and exposing the failure of the public works.

Others followed the Quakers' example. Many British were genuinely moved by the revelations of Irish conditions and responded generously. In January 1847 the British Association for the Relief of Extreme Distress in Ireland and Scotland was established in London, with government encouragement. Following a contribution of £2000 by Queen Victoria, the fund rose to over £435,000. Many commentators wrote that while immediate assistance was vital, the duty of government was to see that it would not be needed again.

Trevelyan soon began to manipulate the use of British Association funds to bolster his own agenda, but there

In November 1846 the Quaker Central Relief Committee in Dublin began to organize soup kitchens in distressed areas to provide free food for the starving. The Quaker soup house in Cork (above) distributed about 1500 gallons daily in January 1847. Relief aid was channeled to groups of Irish Quakers in the localities and to other humanitarian workers. Turnip and cabbage seed was also distributed.

were other charitable contributions over which he had no such control. Collections were made in all parts of the British Empire, and Irish soldiers serving as far away as India contributed as much as they could. The Protestant and Catholic churches in Britain and abroad organized separate funds for distribution by their Irish colleagues.

America Also Gave Much Assistance

Philanthropic bodies, such as the New England Relief Committee of Boston, collected funds and foodstuffs and arranged for direct shipments across the Atlantic. Over one hundred ships loaded with relief goods worth $545,145 sailed for Ireland and Scotland in 1847. Congress rejected giving direct state aid to Ireland, but made warships available for transporting food.

Tens of thousands of Irish immigrants had arrived in the United States in the decades before the Famine. Acutely aware of the privations and sufferings of relatives and friends, many sent money for general relief or to encourage emigration.

Beginning in 1847, hundreds of thousands of dollars were sent from the United States to Ireland by Irish immigrants in the form of cash and remittance drafts (above).

The USS *Macedonian* (below) arrived at Cork with food aid from New York in the summer of 1847. The use of American warships for charitable purposes— they sailed under white flags with a shamrock wreath around a thistle— caused a stir in Britain and Ireland, but much of this help came too late to prevent mass mortality.

Fever and Disease

Effective aid was slow in reaching remote parts of
Ireland. Relatively few perished directly from starvation,
but malnutrition paved the way for fatal diseases. First
to appear were "social infections." Two strains of fever
were observed: typhus—known as "black fever" because
of the rash that accompanied its effects—and "relapsing"
or "yellow fever," which was accompanied by jaundice.
The latter was usually less fatal, but was more violent
in its symptoms and frequently recurred. Both were
carried by the common louse, which multiplied
as falling income brought a deterioration in
hygiene standards.

Famine was responsible for lowering
people's resistance and creating epidemic
conditions as destitute thousands
thronged to overcrowded worksites
and towns in the hope of finding
food, work, or escape. "Famine
fever" killed not only the poor,
but also many doctors, clergy,
and relief officers who came in
close contact with them. It is
estimated that a million and a
half people contracted fever,
and at least a quarter of a
million of them died during
the Famine.

Above: Famine fevers
killed huge numbers
in 1847. Medical science
offered no remedies; only
the provision of adequate
nutrition before it was
too late could limit the
spread of the disease.

Infectious Diseases Were Also Major Killers

Dysentery, or "bloody flux," was spread by bacilli through bowel discharges, which in turn were often provoked by the consumption of poorly cooked maize. Diarrhea, measles, and tuberculosis became rampant as malnutrition weakened the immune system; they were responsible for up to one-third of all deaths.

Vitamin-deficiency diseases such as scurvy, the eye condition xerophthalmia, and pellagra were also common. Extreme malnutrition led to "famine dropsy" (edema) and the wasting disease marasmus, one of the greatest causes of mortality.

The number of medical facilities in Ireland had been among the best in Europe—a network of hospitals and clinics existed by 1845. But these facilities were often rudimentary and poorly distributed and were overwhelmed as the Famine passed into its second year. Bessborough reestablished a Central Board of Health in early 1847, and considerable efforts were made to create temporary fever hospitals and recruit medical staff, but the system was inadequate. No remedies for fever or dysentery were known, and quarantine was impossible.

"The woman…brought forward her little infant, a thin-faced baby of two years, with clear, sharp eyes that did not blink, but stared stock still at vacancy, as if a glimpse of another existence had eclipsed its vision. Its cold, naked arms were not much larger than pipe straws, while its body was swollen to the size of a full-grown person."
Elihu Burritt
A Visit of Three Days to Skibbereen, 1847

Famine reigned everywhere in the season that was to be remembered as Black '47. Even the relatively prosperous northeastern counties of Antrim and Armagh were racked by death as fever spread there with the streams of refugees from the west. In many places the traditional rituals of wakes, burials, and keening (wailing for the dead) were abandoned as whole families died. Left: A funeral at Skibbereen, January 1847.

Soup Kitchens

In January 1847 the government made an about-face. Russell was now convinced that "the pressing matter at present is to keep the people alive" and that "soup kitchens appear the most immediate relief." The Quakers had proved what was possible and lobbied hard for the government to follow suit. Even Trevelyan and Wood were prepared for a change of direction, if for different reasons. As the public works had failed to stimulate exertion, they now hoped to support the people more directly from local taxes and to prevent further problems by a "cooked food test." Most importantly, the moralists wanted the system to be based on the poor law, to pave the way for a permanent structure in Ireland.

A new relief commission was formed under Sir John Burgoyne, but the new act was not quickly implemented. Russell was aware of the dangers of shutting down the public works before the soup kitchens were ready, but with numbers employed still rising (up to 714,000 in early March), there was intense pressure to cut back on spending and to release laborers for planting.

On 20 March the closings began with the dismissal of one-fifth of the workforce. It was intended to close all the public works by 1 May, but this proved impossible, because of the resistance of many workers and the absence of any alternative relief in areas. However, by the end of June all but 28,000 had been discharged. Some workers rioted against the soup kitchens and the demeaning regime this system entailed.

10th March. 1847

Mr. Soyers

Soup Receipts

for the use of

the Irish poor

Copied with

a view, should an.

Opportunity offer, of

their being used for

the benefit of the poor

Labourers at and about

the Arigna Mines.

County Roscommon

Robert White.

Above: A soup recipe. The commission ordered a daily ration of one pound of meal per adult, generally a mixture of maize, rice, and oats, cooked to produce a "stirabout" weighing three to five pounds. This was thought to be the minimum required to sustain health, but some local committees at first distributed a cheaper "poor soup" that merely added to malnutrition. Left: Stirabout was boiled in large iron cauldrons.

For Thousands the Soup Kitchens Came Too Late

In some of the worst-affected areas, such as Skibbereen, soup kitchens came into operation only in mid-June. Once they were established, further problems arose. The number of rations issued never matched the full extent of destitution. The poor quality and small quantity of the food distributed by many committees added to popular anger.

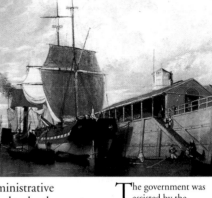

By the first week of July more than three million rations were being distributed daily, at a cost of some two pence per head. In some areas almost the entire population was fed by the state. This extraordinary administrative achievement, despite its flaws, proved to be the most effective means of containing the ravages of famine. It was achieved at a fraction of the cost of the public works: £1,700,000 was spent under the new act (including nearly £1,000,000 in loans that were never repaid).

The soup kitchens proved what the early Victorian state could achieve, even in the worst social conditions. Mortality fell in the summer of 1847 as food was made available where it was needed. Yet the soup kitchens were regarded by the government and British opinion as a strictly temporary measure. In mid-August the soup kitchens began to be phased out, and by the end of September they were all closed.

The government was assisted by the plummeting price of maize in the spring of 1847 due to massive American imports. By late August the cost was less than half that of February. The nature of the Famine began to change, from an absolute shortage of food to a "crisis of entitlements"— the inability of the poor to buy the food that was available. Below: A soup kitchen line in 1847.

"Comprehensive Measures"

Debate raged in the parliamentary session of 1847 over how to deal with Ireland on a permanent basis. One vociferous campaign demanded the extension of the poor law to make localities pay for their own "able-bodied" destitute. The Famine was widely believed to be the result of the land-owners' irresponsibility and indifference to the poor.

Putting the burden of relief on Irish landowners was declared to be the price of British taxpayers' support for the public works and soup kitchens. Ministers like Wood and Grey agreed with this view wholeheartedly; with a general election looming, and signs of a middle-class radical upsurge growing, no one in the Whig government could ignore it.

Some politicians realized that the poor law alone was an inadequate response to Ireland's problems. Lord George Bentinck's bill to spend £16,000,000 on building railways in Ireland fell when it was revealed that most of the money would go to buy land, but Russell later granted £620,000 to existing railway projects. Irish landlords called for a mass program of state-assisted

Above: A caricature of an absentee Irish landlord haunted by the ghosts of his starved tenants. Russell was convinced that the Irish land system must be reformed and drew up a scheme to reclaim the bogs or "waste-lands" for cultivation and settlement by peasant proprietors. This plan was based on the writings of the economist John Stuart Mill and had substantial support in Ireland, but it was rejected by the cabinet and the House of Commons. Russell's hope of resolving Irish poverty through a series of "comprehensive measures" was undermined.

emigration to the colonies, but this proposal was also rejected on the grounds that Ireland could support its present population if they were properly employed.

Only a limited Land Improvement Act was passed to assist the poor law, making loans available to landlords for agricultural "improvements." In practice this law was used only by a few wealthy proprietors who could also draw on English resources.

The Poor Law Extension Act Was Passed in June 1847

The act gave a "right to relief" to the able-bodied poor outside the workhouse, thus making local communities responsible for relieving all local destitution. The fact that Irish landlords led by Lord Monteagle had fought bitterly against the act merely convinced many in Britain and Ireland of its desirability.

Yet the government made major concessions to the landed interest to get the bill through Parliament. Most notoriously, it accepted William Gregory's amendment to deny relief to any tenant holding more than a quarter-acre of land. The consensus was that any tenant unable to support his family should become a landless laborer. Irish landlords were to prove ruthless in using this clause to clear their estates of "surplus" people.

Those ministers who were most convinced of their interpretation of the Famine crisis and who were closest to British public opinion were increasingly setting the policy agenda. For Wood, it was now time for Ireland's regeneration "through a purgatory of misery and starvation."

Daniel O'Connell (idealized in the engraving above) had been ill since the end of 1846 and appeared as a shadow of his former self during his last parliamentary speech early in 1847, during which he appealed in vain for more aid to Ireland. He died while on a pilgrimage to Rome in May 1847, leaving the Irish Catholic community leaderless. His funeral in Dublin (left) was attended by thousands. Lord Lieutenant Bessborough, who had also sought higher relief spending, died in the same month. Irish politicians had little influence on the making of famine-relief policy and were regarded with suspicion or hostility by many in Britain.

The potato did not fail in the summer of 1847. Many observers outside Ireland took the opportunity to declare that the Famine was over and that Ireland must now rely on its own resources for reconstruction. Yet, as very little seed had been available for planting, the potato crop was meager. There was, in fact, no "recovery" in most of Ireland, and starvation and disease continued to ravage the land.

CHAPTER IV
FROM "RECOVERY" TO REBELLION, 1847–8

Tens of thousands were now expelled from their homes. Land-owners claimed they had no option but to evict tenants who failed to pay their rent, but many saw the Famine as an opportunity to clear the land for more profitable uses. Left: *Evicted* by Lady Butler.

A combination of circumstances convinced many in Britain (and some in the wealthier parts of Ireland) that the situation had changed for the better. Trevelyan observed that, since the blight had "shown its teeth without biting too hard," the 1847–8 season was not subject to any specific visitation of Providence and that exceptional aid was therefore unjustified. Reports of an excellent Irish grain harvest and continuing massive imports of American food hardened this consensus. Attempts to raise more money in October met with indifference or outright hostility.

The political balance now also swung decisively in favor of Trevelyan, Wood, and the "moralist" ideologues. The general election of July 1847 was marked by speeches denouncing the "waste" of British taxpayers' money in Ireland, and the parliamentary balance of power passed to a group of middle-class radicals eager to cut expenses. The weak Whig ministry was obliged to give greater weight to the demands of this group following a financial crisis in the autumn of 1847.

The Belief that Ireland Had Returned to Some Sort of "Normality" Bore No Relation to Reality

While the grain harvest had indeed brought some improvement for the farmers of the east and north, it offered only the most temporary respite for the masses of landless laborers and land-poor peasants, particularly in the west. The potato economy had collapsed completely and there was desperately little work available. Smallholders had no realistic alternative to the potato, as most lacked the resources to purchase any other seed. Despite its exhortations

This caricature (below), showing the potato restored to health and hand-in-hand with cheap bread, reflected British complacency about the food situation in the autumn of 1847.

to grow "green crops," the government had refused to distribute more than a token amount of turnip and cabbage seed in 1847 and relied on the landlords or the Quakers to do so.

A combination of harvest employment and population migration allowed the soup kitchens to be dismantled without major unrest, but the cruelty and folly of leaving Ireland to the poor law alone was soon demonstrated.

The Poor Law in Crisis

As people's resources evaporated, large numbers began to flock to the workhouses. Popular loathing for these "Bastilles of the poor" remained intense, but desperation for food, or in the last resort for a decent funeral, forced the destitute to overcome their hatred of the rigid regime and their fear of contagious diseases, which spread rapidly in the workhouses.

By October 1846 many workhouses were full, but continued to squeeze people in. Boards of guardians rented emergency accommodation, but this never kept up with demand. Many felt they had little choice but to give "outdoor" relief (outside the workhouse) in food and ignored official attempts to ban this practice.

The Poor Law Was Again Saddled with the Weight of Relief in October 1847

Efforts were now made to use incarceration as a "test of destitution" for those fit to work. Workhouse accommodation was expanded over the following years to impose this "discipline" on the poor. Over 150,000 places were available by September 1848, rising to about 250,000 a year later. Even this number was far from sufficient in winter and spring, the seasons of greatest distress. However, the majority of inmates remained those too sick to be removed, along with thousands of orphaned or abandoned children.

The boards of guardians were obliged to raise and collect taxes sufficient to alleviate distress. Many guardians, facing strong resistance from landowners and farmers and pessimistic about their district's capacity to pay, were

An industrial depression following the collapse of railway and corn speculation brought distress to the British poor from 1847 to 1849 (opposite above). High taxation was attacked and *The Times* condemned any further British aid to Ireland as an unfair burden on England and a "misplaced humanity," inhibiting Irish self-reliance.

Russell (above) proposed a series of Irish "permanent improvements" from 1847 to 1849, including harbor building, wasteland drainage, and a "colonization" of Canada with railroad-building work for emigrants on arrival. He was too weak to win support for his ideas.

reluctant to comply. Where boards refused, they were replaced by appointed vice-guardians who carried out the collections with military and police assistance. Thirty-nine boards were suspended in 1847–8. Appointed officials administered these rigidly, but professionally.

The system was already under severe pressure by the end of 1847. In December the Irish poor law commissioners had to authorize outdoor relief to the able-bodied unemployed. By June 1848 over 800,000, about two-fifths of whom were able-bodied, were on outdoor relief. The cause of this was clear: There was insufficient work available for many thousands. Even for those incapable of heavy work, outdoor relief was accompanied by harsh conditions. The commissioners insisted that food be distributed in the form of cooked rations, in the interests of economy and nutrition. If the soup-kitchen network of summer 1847 had been retained, this might have been effective, but local boards lacked the administrative machinery and money, and food depots were fewer in number.

The destitute thus had either to squat in the towns and surrounding countryside, where they were prey to epidemic diseases, or travel long distances for food that could spoil on the return journey. Exhaustion and bad winter weather whittled down the numbers who made such treks. The consequences were predictable in such areas as the remote barony of Erris in northwest Mayo, which was over forty miles from the nearest workhouse

Inadequate provision for fever-sufferers ensured that disease spread rapidly in the cramped workhouses, and mortality reached appalling levels by early 1847. In March the Skibbereen workhouse —which had been built for 800—held 1449 people and had a weekly death rate of about 85. A high proportion of inmates were orphaned children. Above: Workhouse orphans. Below: An orphaned girl at Crossmolina, County Mayo.

at Ballina. Here, 10,000 were said to be "starving on turnip tops, sand-eels, and sea-weed, and not even enough of this."

Administrators and Politicians

The poor law officials—from chief commissioner Edward Twisleton to the inspectors and vice-guardians in the field —were mostly conscientious individuals, though they were constrained by the crude administrative thinking of the day. They recognized that the system was collapsing and argued that inadequate funds lay at the root of the problem. It was simply impossible to recover enough local taxes, which in the west exceeded a quarter of the nominal valuation of the land and were widely resisted or evaded.

Lord Clarendon, the new Lord Lieutenant, was soon converted to the view that, without additional resources, suffering would soon push the people into rebellion. He pleaded with the Treasury that they could not "allow above a certain number" to starve. Trevelyan responded by designating twenty-two unions in Connacht and along the western seaboard as "distressed" enough to deserve assistance from the remaining British Association funds. This aid was pitifully inadequate, but further calls from the Irish administration for greater spending were ignored.

What Explained This Callous Indifference in the Face of Human Catastrophe?

Motives went deeper than a desire not to "transfer" famine from Ireland to England. Moralist politicians and British public opinion believed that Ireland was teeming with resources that required only entrepreneurship and industry to be released. The purpose of the poor law was to implement this theory. The horrific consequences of such rigid thinking were either ignored or blamed on the Irish.

The destitute poor far outnumbered the capacity of the workhouses and many were relieved "out of doors." Those deemed "able-bodied" (capable of work) were obliged to break stones for up to ten hours a day. This pointless exercise was deeply hated, but officials insisted that any more productive work would interfere with the labor market. The work test was rigidly enforced, and those absent from roll calls were often removed from the relief lists. Above: Clifden workhouse. Below: *The Stonebreaker.*

Evictions

The government's reliance on landowners to provide employment and relief was misplaced. Most proprietors believed the Malthusian doctrine that Ireland was grossly overpopulated and that only a thinning of the population and strict social control over the remainder would create the necessary conditions for agricultural development. The majority, who regarded themselves as humane and responsible, looked to mass emigration to solve the problem and believed that only the state had the resources to implement emigration on a sufficient scale. As it became clear that the state would intervene only to ensure that landowners paid their share of the mounting debts and taxes for poor relief, many felt themselves justified in evicting their tenants.

Middle range and small farmers were unable to pay the wages previously given to laborers in the form of potato ground and were squeezed after the summer of 1847 by the rising demands for poor taxes. Such intense pressure promoted a ruthless disregard for those lower in the social scale than themselves, as well as a resistance to landlord demands for rent. Saving enough for a passage across the Atlantic and establishing their families in America became their overwhelming concern. Farmers often evicted their own subtenants before being "cleared" themselves.

For cottiers holding only a few acres, the situation was much worse. Landlords were obliged by law to pay the poor taxes of tenants with holdings valued under £4 annually, and most regarded this class with contempt as a parasitic encumbrance. After 1846 most landlords were unwilling to allow rent abatements.

Evictions Soared in 1847

Waves of "clearances," or mass evictions, increased in the following years, especially in the western counties of Clare and Mayo. National figures were not collected until 1849, but they give some idea of the scale of the campaign. Between 1849 and 1854 nearly 50,000 families (about a quarter of a million people) were permanently evicted from their homes.

Landlord strategy was ruthless. The evicted were usually turned out on the road by bailiffs supported by the police and army. Cottages were "tumbled" (pulled down) by the landlord's "crowbar brigade," and sanctions were imposed on any neighboring tenant who sheltered the evicted families. At best, landowners would give the evicted a few pounds compensation for peaceful surrender or allow them to carry away their thatched roofing.

Above: Bridget O'Donnell and her children, evicted from their cabin near Kilrush, County Clare, in 1849.

The evicted, who were extremely reluctant to enter the disease-ridden workhouses, often sought refuge in temporary shelters erected by the sides of roads, until they were eventually removed by coercion, desperation, or death. For many, such as the remnants of the 150 families evicted from the Walsh estate in Erris, who arrived as "living skeletons" to beg in Belmullet in late 1847, clearance was a death sentence.

The records of evictions represent only a portion of those removed from their homes. Very large numbers were made to surrender their holdings "voluntarily" in order to obtain poor law relief under the terms of the notorious "quarter-acre clause." Many proprietors took advantage of the situation to insist (illegally) that applicants pull down their cabins before receiving relief. Small sums were given in compensation to those who cooperated. Even so, a considerable number of smallholders chose to risk starvation rather than surrender their land. Twisleton pleaded that the law be amended to allow the families of these tenants to receive workhouse relief, but the government made only minor concessions.

A minority of Irish proprietors, such as George Henry Moore, also a Member of Parliament, who refused to carry out evictions on his Galway estate, acted humanely during the Famine. Most, however, either pursued their own self-interest or were powerless to act because of the debts, mortgages, and encumbrances on their estates. Wealthy absentee landlords with British resources were often in a better position to help, but most were indifferent and left their Irish agents to deal harshly with the crisis. Above: *Notice to Quit* (c. 1862) by Erskine Nicol.

By 1847 landlords with many small tenants found it impossible to collect more than a fraction of the rent and arrears owed to them. Cottier tenants held more than eighty-five percent of Lord Sligo's estate in County Mayo. Faced with heavy debts to the Westport union and huge encumbrances on his property, Lord Sligo, like many others, claimed he was "under the necessity of ejecting or being ejected" and issued thousands of eviction notices. His neighbor, Lord Lucan, removed 2000 people from the single parish of Ballinrobe alone, converting the cleared land into pasture. Evicted families often constructed temporary shelters from the debris of their "tumbled" cabins, known as "scalpeens." The even less fortunate dug "scalps"— holes two to three feet deep, covered with sticks or turf. They were eventually forcibly removed from these hovels, and many of those evicted in Mayo during 1848 were reported to have died on the roadsides. Left: *An Irish Eviction* (1850) by Frederick Goodall.

"Perhaps in no instance does the oppression of the poor…come before the mind so vividly, as when going over the places made desolate by the famine, to see the tumbled cabins, with the poor, hapless inmates, who had for years sat around their turf fire, and ate their potatoe together, now lingering and oftimes wailing in despair, their ragged bare-foot little ones clinging about them, one on the back of the weeping mother, and the father looking in silent despair, while a part of them are scraping among the rubbish to gather some little relic of mutual attachment…then, in a flock, take their solitary, pathless way to seek some rock or ditch, to encamp supperless for the night." This description of evictions near Newport, County Mayo, 1848, is taken from Asenath Nicholson, *Lights and Shades of Ireland*, 1850. Left: *The Eviction* (c. 1853) by Erskine Nicol.

Agrarian Agitation

Landlord brutality occasionally met with a violent response. At the end of 1847 the number of so-called "outrages" linked to agrarian disputes rose rapidly, and a number of landlords and tenants were murdered. Landowners demanded additional repressive powers.

While murders were rare in the very poorest parts of the west, where food rather than land was the most immediate concern, disturbances spread throughout much of central Ireland in 1847–8. Clarendon expressed his alarm at the situation and the government responded with the Crime and Outrage Act, which strengthened the powers of police and magistrates. Violence subsided during 1848 under the combined influence of coercion, physical exhaustion, and continued emigration. Many landlords abused the new powers to facilitate the "distraint" (seizure) of goods for rent.

Over much of eastern and northern Ireland, tenant farmers turned to less violent tactics. Tenant societies

The Famine inevitably sharpened conflicts not only between landlord and tenant but also within the "peasant" community itself. Previously "comfortable" farmers, who also found themselves facing destitution, sought to defend what little they still had against the tax collectors and the poorer cottiers and laborers. Traditions of mutual assistance often collapsed in the struggle for survival. Below: A farming family defending their home in 1847.

The romantic nationalism preached by Thomas Davis in *The Nation* became popular in 1842. This Young Ireland newspaper was often read aloud to the illiterate (left). However, the Young Ireland intellectuals failed to recruit a mass following before 1848, except among the artisans of Dublin and other large towns.

Below: Scattered groups of uprooted laborers took to "brigandage"—raiding food convoys and farms —in the mountainous areas. Their numbers were always exaggerated by the British press.

sprang up demanding rent reductions and "fixity of tenure" (the right to stay on one's holding as long as a "fair rent" was paid). Russell and Clarendon favored some concession to the demands of these "respectable" tenants and considered granting a form of "tenant right." Yet orthodox thinking again proved too influential in England, and these proposals were abandoned. Landlords only considered reducing rents when large numbers of better-off farmers began emigrating in 1849.

Young Ireland

Following O'Connell's death in 1847, his political network degenerated into competing factions, and political leadership passed to the Catholic hierarchy. The bishops frequently condemned state policy, but were divided over how to proceed. Indeed, they were often preoccupied with their own dioceses, where many parish priests were on the verge of destitution.

The Young Ireland nationalists, who had

The French revolution of February 1848 convinced Young Ireland that it was possible to overthrow tyranny without major bloodshed. Although the revolutionary government in Paris refused to give them assistance, and little help was forthcoming from the United States or the radical English Chartists, the Young Irelanders were swept along by revolutionary optimism. Left: An allegory of the "springtime of the nations" (1848).

rejected O'Connell's rapprochement with the Whigs in 1846, felt vindicated by events. All their predictions about the inveterate hostility of Britain to Irish interests appeared correct, and mass mortality seemed to render O'Connell's distaste for bloodshed irrelevant. Yet the Young Irelanders remained on the margins of Irish politics until 1848. Reconciliation with the O'Connellites proved impossible, and the Church was hostile.

In 1847 James Fintan Lalor wrote a series of articles calling for a social revolution of tenant against landlord. Only by "repealing the conquest," he wrote, could Ireland be made free. Lalor's career as

SMYTH

a practical agitator was unsuccessful, but he won the support of the charismatic John Mitchel and many radical Young Irelanders. Mitchel's call for a rent and tax strike in late 1847 led to an open split between radicals and moderates.

Young Ireland renamed itself the Irish Confederation, and in early 1848 began planning for rebellion. In response, Clarendon was given draconian powers and had Mitchel arrested and convicted of treason-felony by a "packed" jury in May. The Confederation had reached a position where it was impossible to withdraw from its promised insurrection, despite poor preparation. The suspension of habeas corpus in July removed the last reservations. As troops swarmed into Dublin and arrests began, William Smith O'Brien and his lieutenants traveled to Tipperary and attempted to raise a popular revolt in the southern countryside.

The Young Ireland rebellion broke out at Ballingarry, County Tipperary, on 29 July 1848. It was a shambles. Crowds of country people assembled to hear the Confederate leader William Smith O'Brien declare war, but they faded away when it became clear that no food would be distributed. The rising ended in a clash between less than a hundred poorly armed insurgents and a party of police in the "Widow McCormack's cabbage patch" (below). The rebels were soon dispersed by crown forces, and although several Young Irelanders sought refuge with bands of agrarian rebels in the hills, the uprising was effectively over.

The Consequences of the Uprising

The government avoided making martyrs of the leaders convicted of treason by transporting them to Van Diemen's Land (Tasmania) instead of executing them. The Young Irelanders who escaped to America or France remained convinced of the justice of their cause and soon became leaders of the Irish community abroad, which was swollen by thousands of Famine exiles. Many concluded that ardor was no substitute for military preparation in planning an insurrection.

Not all former Young Irelanders remained on the revolutionary path. Charles Gavan Duffy revived *The*

William Smith O'Brien arrested at Thurles railway station (left) and in prison at Clonmel (above, seated). A Protestant landowner and Member of Parliament, Smith O'Brien led Young Ireland from 1846 and, with Charles Gavan Duffy and John Blake Dillon, believed it possible to recruit the "patriotic gentry" to the nationalist cause by taking their side against the government. They adopted a socially conservative approach in the misplaced hope that they would win over the landlords and were skeptical about the idea of tenant revolt. Smith O'Brien was deported in 1848, but he was pardoned and returned to Ireland in 1856.

Nation newspaper in 1849 and devoted himself to peaceful agitation for land reform before he emigrated to Australia in 1855. He later pursued a political career that secured him a knighthood and the premiership of the state of Victoria in 1871.

On his return to Ireland in 1856, Smith O'Brien was a moderating force in Irish nationalism. John Blake Dillon went further, and associated himself with the plans of the British Liberal politician W. E. Gladstone for Irish reform in 1865.

The uprising of 1848 had been a mixture of blind revolutionary optimism and despair at the state of Ireland. It did nothing to improve the lot of the poor and merely hardened the British conviction that the Irish were ungrateful and inveterately violent.

The diarist Charles Greville noted in the summer of 1848 that the dominant feeling in London was "disgust…at the state of Ireland and the incurable madness of the people."

Several leaders evaded arrest in 1848 and fled to the United States. There they were joined by John Mitchel, who escaped from Tasmania in 1853. The more radical émigrés devoted themselves to continuing the struggle for Irish freedom and rejected the moderation and openness that they blamed for the failure of 1848. Involvement in American politics distracted and divided the group, but they went on to found the Fenian movement in the late 1850s. Below: *The Captured Mitchelite*, as imagined by the *Historic Times* in 1849.

Any illusion that the Famine was over was dispelled by the reappearance of the potato blight, "more mysterious than ever," in 1848. Cruelly, the disease was now concentrated in areas least able to bear a fourth year of food shortage. As conditions began to improve in the less-impoverished districts, the west and south were subjected to horrors equaling those of Black '47. Additional potato failures in 1849 and 1850 prolonged the agony of some areas for several years.

CHAPTER V
RELAPSE, 1848–51

The Irish Famine (1849–50) was one of four emblematic works in which the painter George Frederic Watts expressed anger at contemporary poverty and injustice.

The blight returned in July 1848. Officials estimated that about half the total potato crop was lost and that in the west the disaster equaled that of 1846. Clarendon grasped the catastrophic consequences for the poor in that region, whose "constitutions are so broken that they are more than half rotten from all they have gone through" and who had "been feeding more on hope than on meal." They would "now die in swarms."

The Agony of the West

The poor law was no more ready to meet the renewed crisis than it had been the previous year. The numbers on outdoor relief climbed steadily to reach 784,000 in July 1849. A further 250,000 were crammed into the workhouses, and more rioted at the gates for what little relief there was. Many of these applicants were small farmers ruined by the potato failure and the crushing weight of poor taxes.

The figures give little sense of the conditions suffered by those on relief, and none of those beyond its reach. The specter of death from starvation or famine-related disease again stalked the land. Average weekly mortality rates in the workhouses rose from 2.5 per thousand in September 1848 to 12.4 per thousand in May 1849. This translates into some 2500 deaths per week nationally in early 1849.

In the distressed union of Ennistymon, County Clare, the weekly death rate was a staggering fifty-two per thousand by December 1848. More than half the deaths took place within two months of admission, which suggests that it was less the workhouse conditions than the destitution and disease ravaging the population outside that was responsible. It was impossible to count the numbers dying outside the workhouses, but in the west they may even have surpassed the devastation of 1846–7.

Poor law unions slid further into debt as poverty swamped local resources. By January 1849, out of the

"Searching for potatoes [above] is one of the occupations of those who cannot obtain outdoor relief. It is gleaning in a potato field—and how few are left after the potatoes are dug, must be known to every one who has ever seen the field cleared. What the people were digging and hunting for, like dogs after truffles, I could not imagine, till I went into the field, and then I saw them patiently turning over the whole ground, in the hopes of finding the few potatoes the owner might have overlooked…it is the only means by which the gleaners could hope to get a meal."

The Illustrated London News, 22 December 1849

80,000 people in the Skibbereen union, 19,200 were on relief, at an unsustainable cost. As the national relief expenditure soared to £2,200,000 in the season of 1848–9, the imposition of even higher poor taxes offered no solution. Faced with financial collapse, poor law officials vainly implored London for assistance.

Potato Crop Figures 1844–9

Potato acreage
Acres planted with potatoes (millions)

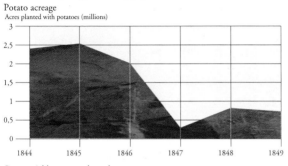

Potato yield per acre planted (figures for 1844-46 estimates)
Potato yield per acre (in tonnes)

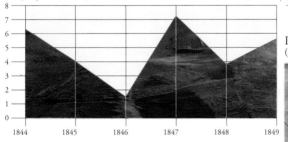

Total produce of potatoes (figures for 1844-46 estimates)
Produce (millions of tonnes)

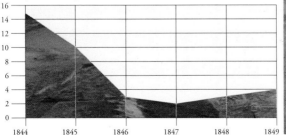

The arrival in November 1848 of the cholera pandemic which had swept across Europe made matters still worse in Ireland. In areas recovering from famine conditions, such as Belfast, a relatively effective medical response was possible, but in the west, containment and treatment proved impossible because of the absence of funds. Cholera spread through contaminated water supplies, which were prevalent in the over-crowded workhouses, market towns, and ports. By the time the disease had exhausted itself in the summer of 1849, thousands of the most vulnerable had perished.

Potato usage
(pre-Famine) :

Export 2%
Wastage 5%

Seed 13%

Animal food 33%

Human food 47%

"Hunted off the Land": The Clearances Continued

In 1848 and 1849 the Kilrush union of west Clare became most notorious for ruthless landlord behavior and was the subject of a parliamentary inquiry. The outraged reports of Captain Arthur Kennedy, the local poor law inspector, made grim reading. Nearly 7000 were evicted in this union in the six months before February 1849, and the process continued thereafter at a rate of some 150 per week. The continuation of such mass expulsions combined with the persistence of potato blight in Clare to render famine distress endemic in this county until 1852–3.

Corruption Exposed

Workhouse conditions in the west deteriorated further in the spring of 1849 as salaried vice-guardians were replaced by elected boards. Some of these were responsible and humane, but too many abused their powers

Above: The village of Tullig, near Kilrush, as drawn by an artist from *The Illustrated London News* in late 1849. "The sketch is not of a *deserted village*…for wretched beings who once viewed it as an abode of plenty and peace still linger and hover about it—but of a destroyed village."
The Illustrated London News, 15 December 1849

A watercolor of boys at an evangelical "soup school" in the west of Ireland (left). Such private "missionary" establishments distributed free food to children who attended Protestant classes.

When state relief failed, the poor became dependent on the whims of private philanthropy. Below: The provision of relief for the evicted of Kilrush, November 1849. "Miss Kennedy (about seven years old) is the daughter of Captain Kennedy, the Poor-Law inspector of the Kilrush Union. She is represented as engaged in her daily occupation of distributing clothing to the wretched children brought around her by their more wretched parents. In the front of the group I noticed one woman crouched like a monkey, and drawing around her the only rag she had left to conceal her nudity…"

The Illustrated London News, 22 December 1849

at the expense of the destitute. The scale of corruption was revealed by the philanthropist Sidney Godolphin Osborne, who visited the west in 1849 and 1850.

In the Limerick and Clifden unions, Osborne found a "wanton contempt for life and decency" and a cynical evasion of the rules laid down in the "Green Book" of workhouse regulations. He denounced merchants who sought election as guardians only to cream off the lucrative contracts for supplies and who then failed to deliver. Such behavior was tolerated, Osborne lamented, because "humanity…has been so taxed, that it has become blind to anything, which might increase its burdens." In the meantime, women and children—who formed the bulk of the inmates—languished in idleness and despair.

"Souperism"

One of the enduring images of the Famine is

the use of relief for religious proselytizing. Catholics who converted were denounced as "jumpers," or, because the material motivation of food relief was suspected, as "soupers."

Such activity was less widespread than might be expected: Proselytizing was banned from state relief and shunned by such altruistic groups as the Quakers. Many local Protestant and Presbyterian clergy also refused to exploit the situation and often worked selflessly and in collaboration with their Catholic counterparts for the good of their parishes.

Yet "souperism" did occur and may have been more prominent in the later years of the Famine as state relief dried up. Protestant evangelical societies had set up missionary "colonies" in remote parts of Ireland before the Famine: The best known were on Achill Island in Mayo and at Dingle in Kerry. British evangelicals continued to channel funds into such settlements in the late 1840s. The existence of such well-provisioned centers in the midst of mass destitution inevitably attracted those in extreme need.

The Catholic perception of the Protestant clergy as parasites, living off tithes while the people starved, added to a lasting sense of sectarian bitterness. Above: A vicious caricature from 1847 shows the devil presiding over a clerical feast while the people starve. Below: An evicted cottier at Kilrush.

The Failure of Relief

By the end of 1848 the wells of private charity had run dry, and Ireland staggered through the winter of 1848–9 without any substantial aid. The final blow came in June 1849, when the Quakers abandoned their work, commenting that "the Government alone could raise the funds and carry out the measures necessary in many districts to save the lives of the people."

The urgent demands for more money sharpened the government's divisions. Wood and Grey held firm to their insistence on "letting things take their course." Faced with a British refusal to allow any but the smallest grants for Ireland, Russell introduced early in 1849 a rate-in-aid, which would tax the eastern and northern parts of Ireland to support the starving west. It was deeply resented in Ulster, where there was now little sympathy for the "feckless" paupers of the west. It was also denounced by many landowners as a denial of the shared responsibilities of the Union.

Most poor law officers agreed that the Famine was an "imperial" disaster and that further burdens should not be placed on Ireland alone. Twisleton resigned in March 1849 on the grounds that "the destitution here is so horrible, and the indifference of the House of Commons to it so manifest, that he is an unfit agent of a policy that must be one of extermination."

Reforms to the poor law in 1849 made minor concessions to the landlords' clamor for change but did nothing for the destitute. Trevelyan clung to his ideological obsessions, rejecting intervention on the grounds that "what the patient now requires is rest and quiet and time for the remedies which have been given to operate." In 1850 Russell was able to extract only a further £300,000 loan and a rescheduling of debts. Often he too lapsed into fatalistic

The vote of a small relief grant of £50,000 in February 1849 met with outrage in Britain. *The Times* thundered that it "has almost broken the back of English benevolence.… We believe the great reason to be the total absence not merely of gratitude, but the barest 'receipt' for all these favors." Below: A caricature of John Bull about to throw off his troublesome Irish burden.

rationalizations or recriminations against the Irish, and he ultimately agreed with Clarendon's despairing comment that "the wretched people seem to be human potatoes, a sort of emanation from 'the root'—they have lived by it and will die with it."

"Free Trade in Land"

By 1849 many in England looked to "free trade in land" as the panacea for Ireland. The idea of opening land ownership to market forces caught the liberal imagination and blended with the widespread criticism of the existing landlords. Middle-class radicals and politicians like Charles Wood, who adopted their free-trade attitudes, believed that Ireland needed a "clearance," or large-scale eviction, of its proprietors and their replacement by British middle-class "yeomen." Such newcomers were expected to introduce capital and entrepreneurial values.

Large numbers of estates were bankrupt even before the Famine. Sales were impeded by complex legal charges and entails on the land, and mortgagors were often content with the steady income extracted by agents from the rack-rented (subject to excessive rents) tenants. The Famine threw more landlords into insolvency, but many tried to cling to their land because of the low price of property. Legal obstruction nullified attempts to introduce reforms in 1847 and 1848.

The 1849 Encumbered Estates Act created a special court with compulsory powers to force the sale of estates. It was very active in the following years—selling 917 estates by April 1853 —but it did not have the

A caricature mocking "little" John Russell's visit to Ireland in September 1848 (below left). This was another abortive attempt to construct a remedial policy. The parliamentary reformer Russell concluded that the problem was the anti-Irish hostility lying "deep in the breasts of the British people."

anticipated effect. Just four percent of purchasers came from outside Ireland, and, although some lots were bought by middle-class Irish Catholics, most of the land was redistributed among the existing Anglo-Irish landowning families. Only a handful of British farmers were persuaded to cross the water to manage or lease the new large grazing farms created by mass evictions.

The Queen's Visit

Clarendon hoped a "private" visit by Queen Victoria would stabilize the political situation, promote investment in Irish land and mark a symbolic "end" to the Famine. It was the first royal visit to the country since 1821. The royal party landed in August 1849 at Cork, Dublin, and Belfast, with only a brief foray into the Kildare countryside. The Ireland the queen saw was the recovering part; once again the shattered west was forgotten.

In 1849 Peel proposed a relief plan for the Irish west featuring its "plantation" by British farmers. Peel's suggestions for spending more on relief works did not get far, but his speeches revived the idea of "free trade in land." This caricature (opposite) shows Ireland starving, while Russell and Peel sow their schemes.

Below: Queen Victoria and her family at Kingstown (Dun Laoghaire) Harbour.

Despite the re-emergence of republicanism in 1848, Queen Victoria was not personally unpopular in Ireland. O'Connell had always been anxious to demonstrate Irish loyalty to a monarch who appeared free of her ancestors' anti-Catholic prejudices. The young queen landed first at Cove, which was renamed Queenstown in her honor, before going on to Cork by steam launch. The royal party later sailed to Dublin and Belfast and was greeted with enthusiasm in the eastern cities, where considerable amounts of money had been spent on welcoming celebrations. The queen saw little of the interior, except for a short visit to the Duke of Leinster's showpiece estate at Carton, County Kildare, where selected tenants danced jigs for her amusement. The visit stimulated imitative English tourism, but had none of the hoped-for permanent effects, and famine lingered on in Clare and Connacht. Both the queen's attitude to Ireland, and majority feeling towards her in that country were to sour in later years.

Left: The arrival of the queen at Belfast.

Scenes from the queen's visit to Dublin. *The Illustrated London News* described the preparations: "For once, at least, Dublin looked as much like the veritable capital of a great and prosperous kingdom as the most ardent Repealer could desire. Equipages of all descriptions—but little inferior in brilliancy to any that grace Hyde Park in the height of the London season—rolled through Sackville Street.... Architects, builders, gas-fitters, carpenters, painters, decorators, and others found abundant occupation in making preparations for the forthcoming ceremonial and its after festivities.... There was, it is true, an under-current of ill feeling. The Lord Mayor issued a proclamation ...calling on all classes of the inhabitants to illuminate; but, as the proclamation was, after a few days, superseded by another, merely requesting all who could afford to show their loyalty in that way to do so, and exonerating from the implication of disloyalty all who might be too poor to spend money in tallow or gas, the dissatisfaction gradually subsided."

The Cost of the Famine

The 1851 Irish census revealed that the population had fallen to about 6,600,000. When estimates of "natural" growth are taken into account, the "missing" total some 2,400,000, or more than a quarter of the country's population. Sorting the number of emigrants from the dead is difficult, but recent research suggests that Famine mortality was around 1,100,000.

Whom did the Famine kill? Not surprisingly, the poor suffered worst, as they were most vulnerable to destitution. However, large numbers of doctors, clergy, and relief workers also died from epidemic disease. Slightly more men than women were killed, but it was the very young (under five years old) and the elderly (over forty years old) who were most likely to die.

The response of the British government to the Irish catastrophe was grossly inadequate, particularly after the autumn of 1847. From 1845 to 1850 the Treasury spent £8,100,000 on relief, of which just over half was in loans to be repaid by Ireland. When the remaining debts were cancelled in 1853, the net amount spent

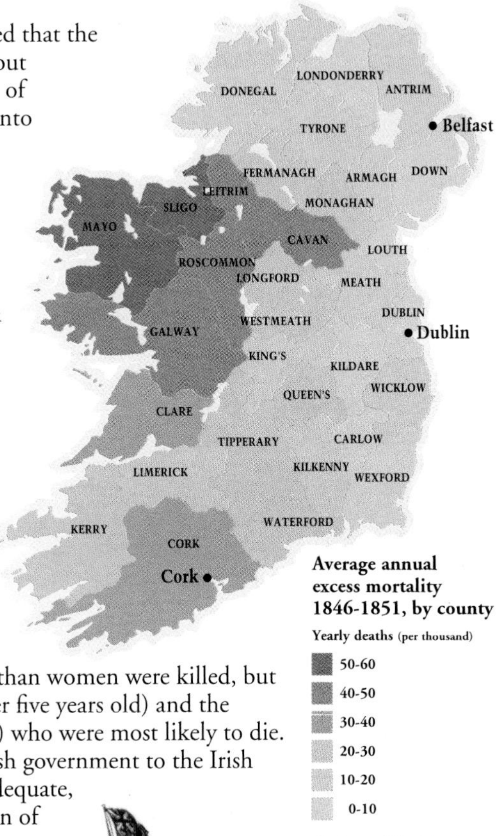

Average annual excess mortality 1846–1851, by county

Yearly deaths (per thousand)

- 50-60
- 40-50
- 30-40
- 20-30
- 10-20
- 0-10

A bove: The Famine was a national catastrophe but was mixed in its regional impact. "Excess" mortality was very high in the rural far west, high in Munster and south Ulster, and low in east Ulster and Dublin. Left: An American cartoon criticizing the poverty and violence of Irish immigrants.

was some £7,000,000, representing less than half of one percent of the British gross national product over five years. Contemporaries noted the sharp contrast with the £20,000,000 compensation given to West Indian slaveowners in the 1830s. Historians have pointed to the even more marked discrepancy with the nearly £70,000,000 subsequently spent on the Crimean War of 1854–6. In the event, more money was raised in Ireland than in Britain to meet the cost of the Famine. Poor taxes and landlord borrowing raised over £8,500,000, straining the country's resources to their limit.

In the summer of 1847 the government proved that it could create administrative structures capable of reducing the death rate. The falling price of imported food from this time made effective intervention feasible. In 1849 Edward Twisleton testified that "comparatively trifling sum[s]" were required for Britain "to spare itself the deep disgrace of permitting any of [its] miserable fellow subjects to die of starvation." That more was not in fact spent on keeping people alive was due to the triumph of ideological obsession over humanitarianism.

The population of Ireland fell steadily from 1846 until the 1920s. Some decline in numbers might have occurred without the Famine catastrophe, but it was the scale on which this fall occurred that was so extraordinary. By 1911 Ireland contained 4,390,000 people, just over half the numbers of 1845. Recovery thereafter was slow and concentrated in the industrial regions of Ulster. Continuing high emigration accounts for much of this hemorrhage: Up to five million people left the country in the sixty years after 1851.

POPULATION OF
IRELAND
1841 — 8.196.597
1851 — 6.574.278
1861 — 5.798.967
1871 — 5.409.804
1881 — 5.159.849
Decrease in 40 Years
3.036.748

Emigration from Ireland began long before the Famine, but at the end of 1846 it took on a new and extraordinary character. The following decade saw an unprecedented exodus of about 1,800,000 people, well over a million of these during the Famine years. This population movement was one of the largest during the 19th century in relative terms. For many who left Ireland, more as refugees than voluntary emigrants, it was a searing and horrific experience.

CHAPTER VI

THE EXODUS: EMIGRATION FROM 1846 TO 1855

Many Irish emigrants found it difficult to settle abroad, although very few actually returned to Ireland. *Outward Bound* (opposite) and *Homeward Bound* (right) by Erskine Nicol.

Pre-Famine Emigration

In the 18th century thousands crossed the Atlantic to settle in the American colonies. These early emigrants were disproportionately Presbyterians from the north of Ireland, but also included other Protestants and some Catholics. Interrupted by war, the exodus began again in 1815 and grew in numbers and in the proportion of Catholics. About a million people left Ireland in the thirty years before 1845, mainly for Canada and the United States, but also for the industrializing towns of Great Britain. Some traveled to Australia as well, but the expense restricted this journey to convicts and emigrants who had some financial help.

The majority of emigrants came from the English-speaking and commercialized regions of Ireland. Many of those who went to America were "respectable" farmers and their families, seeking to find in the New World an independence that was increasingly difficult in Ireland. Yet greater numbers of smallholders, cottiers, and farmer's sons also went, assisted by their landlords or by money sent from those who had gone before. The poorest began to adopt the practice of "step migration," taking the cheap steamers to Liverpool or Glasgow in search of jobs that would then finance the trans-Atlantic leap.

The deteriorating economic conditions of the early 1840s encouraged more people to consider emigration, and the practice began to spread to new areas. Fast steamship travel across the Irish Sea and the increased trade between Britain and the Americas reduced the cost of passage. As literacy spread, people became increasingly aware of the methods and possibilities of emigration by reading pamphlets, newspapers, and letters from previous emigrants. Above: A farming family waiting to set sail at Cork, c. 1840. A cross-channel steamer can be seen in the background.

Although more and more Irish wanted to move to the New World, they found it was far from easy. Fares to the United States were still expensive, and few farming families were prepared to go without the savings required to establish a farm. The ocean crossing was potentially perilous and emigrants faced the threat of robbery, fraud, or hostility on arrival. A single negative letter from a friend or relative could dissuade an entire family from making the trip. Priests and nationalist leaders were also ambivalent or even hostile towards emigration, at least in principle.

In some places whole communities took to the road in 1846. Relatively few ships sailed from the west, so most people crossed the island to the eastern ports. Many continued on to Liverpool, the point of departure for most American voyages. Above: An emigrant ship leaving Belfast (1852). Below: Irish emigrants on their way to Cork (1849).

The Famine Exodus

The second potato failure in 1846 caused great alarm. In normal years few dared to cross the Atlantic during the winter storms, but in 1846–7 the fear of starvation drove thousands to take the risk. As cultural restraints broke down and the social structure of rural Ireland collapsed, panic propelled masses of people to the ports. Such traditions as the farewell "emigrant wake" were abandoned, and families were torn apart.

Many had no choice but to leave

if they were evicted from their homes or unable to find employment. However, those from areas with a tradition of emigration or of seasonal migration to Britain for harvest work were the first to go. In places without this tradition, such as southwest Cork, the poor were hesitant to leave and they often died in their own villages as their strength and resources became exhausted.

By the end of 1847 some 230,000 had left for the Americas and Australia, and tens of thousands more had gone to Britain. This was double the number of the previous season, which was itself larger than usual. The rate of emigration tapered off late in 1847, yet it remained relatively high because of money sent by family members or friends to assist those wishing to follow them. In 1849 these sums exceeded £500,000, a figure that had nearly doubled by 1851. Money from abroad facilitated the "chain migration" of entire families and villages, which became a feature of post-Famine Irish emigration.

The potato failure of 1848 provoked another mass exodus. Throngs of people again sought winter passages in 1848–9 and 1849–50, and whole districts were deserted. With larger farmers also cutting their losses and departing, even landlords who had evicted their tenants became alarmed at the "depopulation" of Ireland. In 1849 and 1850 the numbers leaving for America exceeded 200,000 each year. This peaked in 1851 at just under a quarter of a million and then began to decline.

Poorer emigrants in 1847 rarely had sufficient provisions for the Atlantic crossing of about forty days, and lacked the resources to buy the food sometimes sold on board at extortionate prices. Ship captains often refused to issue the rations of food and fresh water laid down by law and ignored basic hygiene precautions. Suffering from seasickness, fever, dysentery, and diarrhea, the huge number of people packed into the "coffin ships" of 1847 were subject to terrible rates of mortality. Below: Emigrants on the docks at Cork.

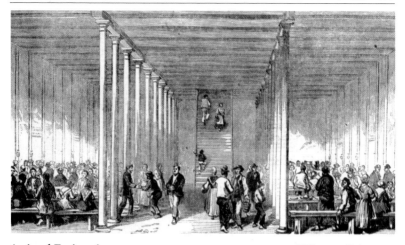

Assisted Emigration

Not all emigrants paid for their own passage. A number of landowners had begun to take unilateral action in assisting tenant emigration before the Famine, and others joined them after the potato failed. Almost all agreed that reducing the population on their estates was necessary for agricultural improvement, but most looked to the state to help remove the people.

The few landowners who did assist were mostly large "improving" proprietors with access to funds or credit outside Ireland; two, Lords Lansdowne and Palmerston, were government officials. All claimed that they were aiding "voluntary" emigrants, but in many cases the only choice given was eviction. Whole communities were shipped from Irish ports in 1846–7, and while conditions were generally better on landlord-chartered ships, many people still died.

Only about 22,000 emigrants were directly assisted by their landlords from 1846 to 1850. For most proprietors, the decision to assist was primarily commercial, although some gave it a paternalistic gloss. Sir Robert Gore Booth spent £15,000 in removing 1340 of his "surplus" tenantry from County Sligo. For the tenants, assisted emigration at least offered an escape from Famine and an opportunity to leave with neighbors and relatives.

There was little state-assisted emigration to Australia at the height of the Famine, and those people sent out later by the emigration commissioners were carefully selected and "balanced" by larger numbers of emigrants from England, Wales, and Scotland. Above: The government emigration depot at Birkenhead in 1852.

Colonization and the Government

Most government officials were convinced that the duty to assist emigration lay with the landowners and were unwilling to meddle with the massive voluntary movement underway from 1847. British radicals continued to argue that Ireland was not overpopulated if the people were put to work and rejected any increased taxation for "colonization." Meanwhile, the British colonies petitioned the government to limit the existing flood of "dangerous" Catholic Irish poor believed to bring disease and disaffection with them.

Lord Grey, the Colonial Secretary, shared Trevelyan's moralism. After toying with a colonization scheme late in 1846, he turned decisively against the idea. By 1848 Russell had become convinced that some project was vital and favored giving emigration aid only to those who worked on a new Canadian railroad linking Halifax and Quebec. Although supported by Clarendon, this plan was smothered.

The only state-assisted emigration in these years took place under the poor law. Guardians were permitted to use the taxes to help destitute emigrants, but little money was available before 1849. Relatively few people, mainly women and children, left the workhouses for Canada in the early 1850s.

The Trans-Atlantic Passage

Liverpool was England's second city, a hub of empire and a thriving commercial port. It was the only center capable of marshaling the shipping demanded by the emigrant flood. The growing trade of British manufactured goods

One controversial emigration scheme involved sending young Irish orphan women to Australia at the expense of the colony, which was believed to be suffering from a "dearth" of females. The plan was voluntary and popular among many young women anxious to escape the poorhouse; over 4000 left by mid-1850. However, the scheme was dogged by "scandals," most involving the unwillingness or inability of the young women from poor rural backgrounds to perform the domestic work allocated to them, and in 1850 it was discontinued. Nevertheless, emigration by unaccompanied young women seeking opportunities denied to them at home became a distinctive feature of post-Famine Irish emigration. Below: Cross-section of an emigrant ship bound for Australia in 1852.

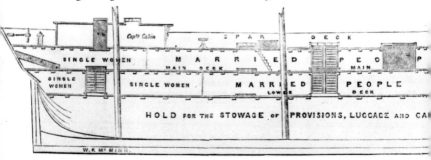

for American farm products boosted the Liverpool–New York traffic, but the cheapest fares were available on the Canadian timberships, which would otherwise have returned empty; their owners were happy to carry human freight.

Passage to British North America (Canada) was difficult in winter while the St. Lawrence River was ice-bound, but in 1847 some 110,000 people left for Quebec, St. John, and other ports. The United States Passenger Acts of 1847, which imposed harsher regulations on emigrant shipping and raised the fare to over £7 per head, encouraged many to take the much cheaper and less-regulated Canadian route, even if the United States was their favored destination.

Shipowners and speculators rushed to cash in on the profits offered by the Irish exodus. Brokers hired any available ship for the purpose and often offered tickets for sale via agents in Ireland. Many small, unseaworthy ships were chartered, and they often managed to evade inspection as passengers embarked at the smaller western ports. These overcrowded, poorly provisioned vessels were the most likely to become "coffin ships"—so-called for their horrendous mortality rates. Brokers preyed on the ignorance and desperation of the Irish poor, who had little idea of what might be needed for the journey or how far away America was.

Most Irish farm laborers had never before traveled more than twenty miles from their homes and many suffered severe disorientation after they left. Some of this dislocation is conveyed in Erskine Nicol's *Irish Emigrant Arriving at Liverpool* (above). Once at Liverpool, emigrants sought lodgings and boat tickets. Swindlers, "runners," and "man-catchers" preyed on the confused, robbing them of baggage and carefully hoarded cash.

Boarding the overcrowded emigration ships of the Famine period was often a chaotic experience. The shipowners and crew believed that the passengers were merely "human freight" and treated them accordingly. The philanthropist Vere Foster, who accompanied Irish emigrants traveling from Liverpool to New York in December 1850 with the intention of exposing the evils of the passenger trade, described the conditions he encountered on boarding the Black Star Line ship *Washington*: "There was no regularity or decency observed with regard to taking the passengers on board the ship; men and women were pulled in any side or end foremost, like so many bundles. I was getting myself in as quickly and dexterously as I could, when I was laid hold of by the legs and pulled in, falling foremost down upon the deck, and the next man was pulled down on top of me." Left: *Emigrant Ship* by Charles Joseph Staniland.

Landing at Grosse Isle

The physical cost of the Famine emigration became evident as ships began to arrive in Canada. Ships bound for Quebec were obliged to stop at the quarantine station at Grosse Isle, about thirty miles down the St. Lawrence. The *Syria*, the first ship of the season, arrived on 14 May 1847, carrying 84 typhus victims out of a total of 241 emigrants. Nine people had already died.

Eight ships arriving in the next four days brought an additional 430 patients. More hospital buildings were commandeered, but many of the sick had to remain aboard ship. By the end of May 40 ships were lined up in the St. Lawrence waiting to unload, while Grosse Isle had over 1100 patients suffering in terrible conditions. It became impossible to isolate the "sick" from the "healthy,"

Medical inspection of emigrants was cursory at Liverpool (above, the inspector's office) and often non-existent at other ports. It was thus inevitable that disease would be brought on to the ships by Famine refugees and that it would incubate in the cramped and insanitary conditions on board. Perhaps one out of five of those traveling to Canada in 1847 died from typhus.

who carried disease with them once released from the island. Many citizens of Montreal and Toronto died as disease spread inland.

By the time the Grosse Isle station was closed at the end of the 1847 sailing season, over 5300 had died there. At least another 15,000 perished soon after landing in British North America. How many died on the voyage and were buried at sea is not recorded, but it is likely that at least five percent of trans-Atlantic passengers perished en route during the Famine years.

The Irish in Canada

Conditions improved in 1848 when Britain responded to Canadian protests with a new Passenger Act that reduced the number of persons a ship could carry. A combination of this act, a punitive immigrant tax, and a recession in the timber trade caused the cost of passage to rise, and consequently emigration to Canada fell to 25,000 in 1848.

Many of those who survived the "plague year" of 1847 and others who arrived later went south to the United States. Some ships merely stopped at Halifax or St. John, New Brunswick, before sailing for Boston or New York. The idea of remaining in a British colony predisposed many to move on, but the recession in the Canadian timber trade and family connections in the United States were also important factors.

A large number did, however, settle in Canada, which had a much higher proportion of Irish-born residents than the United States throughout the 19th century. Until the 1880s the Irish were the largest non-French ethnic group. The better-off often bought small farms and prospered and, while the poorer Irish lacked such opportunities, Canadian nondiscriminatory attitudes promoted integration and hastened an improvement in living standards.

The authorities at Grosse Isle quarantine station were woefully unprepared for the disaster to come; the fever hospital on the island had only 150 available beds. Volunteer doctors and priests did what they could for the dying, but no other port in America saw so many deaths in 1847. Above: *Typhus*, painted at Quebec in 1849.

NOTICE
TO
PASSENGERS & SETTLERS
IN
Canada.

Such Persons in CANADA as are desirous of paying the Passage of their Friends or Relations from IRELAND, are hereby informed, that by depositing the Passage-Money with JAMES BLACK, Esq. QUEBEC, or W. BALDWIN, Esq. NEW YORK, UPPER CANADA, and forwarding their acknowledgment by letter to IRELAND, when presented, Passages to the extent required will be given by

WATSON & GRAVES,

New York and Boston

In 1848 the great majority of Irish began sailing directly to New York. Conditions on the passage to the United States were rarely as bad as those to Canada in 1847, but even on the largest emigrant boats and sailing packets, the crossing could be uncomfortable, tiresome, and dangerous. Although American ships were favored by emigrants, fraud and brutality against passengers were not uncommon. British and American authorities were unable or unwilling to prevent such abuses.

Despite the greater attraction of the United States, Famine immigrants faced difficulties on arrival there. The American authorities had done their utmost to limit the number of Irish immigrants in 1847 by imposing a bonding system, which made shipbrokers

TO EMIGRANTS.

CHOLERA.

CHOLERA having made its appearance on board several Passenger Ships proceeding from the United Kingdom to the United States of America, and having, in some instances, been very fatal, Her Majesty's Colonial Land and Emigration Commissioners feel it their duty to recommend to the Parents of Families in which there are many young children, and to all persons in weak health who may be contemplating Emigration, to postpone their departure until a milder season. There can be no doubt that the sea sickness consequent on the rough weather which Ships must encounter at this season, joined to the cold and damp of an sea voyage, will render persons who are not strong more susceptible to the attacks of this disease.

To those who may Emigrate at this season the Commissioners strongly recommend that they should provide themselves with as much warm clothing as they can, and especially with flannel, to be worn next the Skin; that they should have both their clothes and their persons quite clean before embarking, and should be careful to keep them so during the voyage,—and that they should provide themselves with as much solid and wholesome food as they can procure, in addition to the Ship's allowance to be served on the voyage. It would of course, be desirable, if they can arrange it, that they should not go in a Ship that is much crowded, or that is not provided with a Medical Man.

By Order of the Board,
S. WALCOTT,
Secretary.

On landing, immigrants again had to face gangs of "runners" (above, at New York, in the 1850s), which were usually made up of from their own ethnic group. Baggage was stolen and swindlers regularly cheated those wanting to travel inland.

"Ship fever" (typhus) and cholera were not the only hazards faced by Irish emigrants on the sea-crossing. Fifty-nine passenger ships bound for America were wrecked by storm, fire, and collision in 1847–53, with many fatalities.

or agents responsible for the welfare of their immigrants. But evasion was widespread and attempts to stem the flow across the Canadian border proved hopeless. Boston received over 37,000 Irish emigrants in 1847, increasing its population by one-third and straining its housing, medical, and charitable resources to breaking point. New York, which was much larger, had less difficulty absorbing the 53,000 Irish who landed between May and December 1847, although those released prematurely from the Staten Island quarantine hospital brought disease with them.

Shipbroking firms, such as Tapscott's of Liverpool and New York, grew rich by exploiting the emigrant flood from Ireland. Most companies were unscrupulous in overcrowding their ships and defrauding the passengers. Advertisements (left) were rarely truthful about the size of, or provisions on, the ships.

For immigrants who overcame all these obstacles and reached the American hinterland, material prosperity was possible, but in the Famine generation wealth was restricted mostly to the few who had managed to arrive with savings.

Confused, dispirited, and impoverished, many Irish immigrants got no further than the slum tenements of their port on arrival. Below: The arrival of Irish immigrants at Boston, c. 1850.

Not All Who Fled from Ireland Crossed the Atlantic

Irish laborers had been part of the British workforce for many years, but Famine migrants met with hostility in Britain. They were often the most impoverished, lacking the resources or strength to travel further. Their arrival in large numbers in 1847, particularly in the industrial towns of Lancashire, on Clydeside, and in south Wales and Bristol, seemed to confirm British stereotypes of Irish degradation and created a moral panic. Liverpool was overwhelmed by Irish emigrants in 1847; typhus became rampant, and thousands were supported by the poor taxes.

The English poor law contained a law of settlement, allowing guardians to return the destitute to their place of origin, which was frequently used against the poor Irish. In 1847 about 15,000 were removed from Liverpool, shipped back to Dublin or Cork, and abandoned on the docks. Some Irish who had long resided in the city were also repatriated then. Other British unions followed suit on a smaller scale.

The numbers sent back were a fraction of the hundreds of thousands who arrived in these years. Many went on to London and other towns, but most remained in the northwest of England and Clydeside. By 1851 over one-fifth of the population of Liverpool was made up of Irish Famine migrants.

The Irish Found It Difficult to Assimilate in Britain

Working-class Catholics had at best an ambiguous relationship with British life. Many who had hoped to move on to America or to return to Ireland, having made some money, remained there out of habit or necessity.

Ethnic-religious clashes, such as the notorious Stockport riots of 1852, led many Irish communities to adopt defensive political positions linked to militant Irish

Some Irish Famine migrants lived as farm laborers, dependent on harvest work and begging. Most, however, were drawn to the industrial towns of Great Britain, where they tended to cluster in the same streets and tenements. "Chain migration" encouraged clannishness but much of the Irish population was mobile, moving wherever casual employment became available. Poverty, low social status, and concentration in unskilled occupations continued to characterize the bulk of the Irish in Britain long after the Famine. Although individual experiences varied according to differences of religion, class, and location, in general the Irish suffered under the widespread British prejudice that they were disloyal, stupid, and not able to provide for themselves. They endured much malicious humor and discrimination as a consequence. Left: *Irish Vagrants in England*, painted c. 1853 by Walter Deverell.

nationalism. However, as the Catholic Church began to provide a greater social focus later in the 19th century, it became an instrument for the anglicization of the Irish. The rise of the British Labour Party also promoted Irish integration. Sectarian political, social, and sports rivalries continued to divide Liverpool and Glasgow until recently, but elsewhere the explicit antagonisms of the previous centuries began to fade, at least until the outbreak of the Ulster "troubles" in 1969.

The Irish Diaspora in America

Most Irish immigrants gravitated to the slum quarters of cities, where they could live inexpensively. The vast majority of Famine immigrants became concentrated in the lowest-paid, least-skilled, and most-dangerous occupations available. The number of them in prisons, asylums, and poorhouses was well above average in the following decades. The Irish were highly mobile, but tended to stay with their own people in different cities; disappointment and restlessness were the dominant feelings of many, and early mortality too frequently their fate.

Many of the Irish were ghettoized by the virulent anti-Catholicism of American society, which was exacerbated by the waves of Famine immigration. Irish Orangeism and

Whole regiments of the American army were made up of Irishmen. This recruiting poster, complete with harp and shamrock, is of 1855. During the Civil War thirty-eight Union regiments had the word 'Irish' in their names. (4)

Large numbers of Irish-American men participated in the American Civil War (1861–5). Many volunteered for all-Irish units, but conscription was violently resisted.

Infected ships were obliged to offload their sick at the Staten Island quarantine hospital (below) and remain in quarantine for thirty days before landing at New York. In 1855 Castle Garden on Manhattan was used as an immigrant depot, allowing for more rigorous processing and some protection from "runners." This depot was in turn replaced by Ellis Island in 1892.

American nativism combined to promote discrimination against Catholics of all classes in the 1850s and 1860s. Some emigrants converted or adopted "American" names and habits, but most retreated into the relative safety of Irish-Catholic communities and the institutions that emerged to protect them—the Catholic Church, the Democratic party political machines like Tammany Hall in New York, and the Irish nationalist movement.

Continuing emigration, discrimination, and political interest in the homeland kept the Irish communities abroad self-conscious and vibrant. The Irish in America faced similar problems as the Irish in Britain, but the greater opportunities available in a country of immigrants facilitated gradual social progress. Yet this was not always obvious to those who arrived during the Famine or in the following decades.

Irish immigrants carried with them an image of their homeland that remained frozen in time; for the million and a half who arrived during the Famine and its immediate aftermath, this memory was deeply anti-British. Their feelings were articulated by the exiled Young Irelanders, who rose to the top of Irish-American politics in the 1850s. This elite group of lawyers and journalists shaped the beliefs of the masses, who were organized at a more mundane level by the neighborhood and city "bosses."

An enduring hatred of Britain was the main character-istic of Irish-American nationalism; the popular ballad demanding "revenge for Skibbereen" was typical of its historical obsessions. American fund-raising became a high priority for militant nationalists, all of whom were ready to remind their audiences of the "crime" of the Famine.

Industrializing and expanding America sucked in and exploited cheap unskilled labor, and wherever the factories, railroads, or mines went, the Irish followed. Harsh repression of labor agitation and the popular slogan for skilled jobs: "no Irish need apply," made advance extremely slow. As in other countries, the Irish were at the forefront of labor organization in the 1880s. Above: Construction work on the Union Pacific Railroad, Wyoming, c. 1868.

The Catholic Church: An Irish-American Institution

In the United States the Church was led by dynamic Irish-born bishops from the mid-19th century on, and other Catholic immigrants generally accepted this Irish dominance. As in other countries, the Catholic Church rapidly expanded its programs of education, sports, and social activities at the end of the century. Its growing wealth and respectability were important factors in the rise of the Irish in both American and Australian society.

Over a number of generations, communal action

St. Patrick's Day parade, New York, 1874 (above). Such demonstrations of ethnic identity were important to the political mobilization of immigrant voters. In turn, Democratic party machines brought tangible benefits, such as jobs in the city police force.

Members of the all-Irish 69th New York regiment hear mass during the Civil War (left). Many former soldiers joined the Irish nationalist Fenian movement in the 1860s. For many Irish Americans the fight for Ireland's freedom promised by such organizations was a metaphor for their own struggle to make communal advances in the United States.

and individual perseverance brought prosperity to the Catholic Irish. By 1900 only fifteen percent of Irish-American men remained unskilled workers. Later waves of immigrants from other countries and African Americans from the southern states replaced them at the bottom of the economic pyramid. By the 1920s the Irish had entered virtually every sphere of American life and had started to be absorbed into the mainstream. By the 1960s the Catholic Irish ranked among the country's highest income earners.

A yearning for identity kept the Irish-American community distinct, but its often sentimentalized image of the "old country" was sharply at odds with the reality of a changed Ireland and was losing meaning by the 1960s. Only recently has interest in Irish culture and history begun to revive and develop in new and vibrant ways. The rise of interest in genealogy and the influx in the 1980s of another wave of young Irish immigrants, many of them initially illegal, have contributed to this regeneration of Irish America.

The election of John F. Kennedy, the descendant of Famine emigrants from Counties Wexford and Kerry, as president in 1960 symbolized a "coming of age" for Catholic Irish America. He made a state visit to Ireland in 1963. Below: Kennedy meets the Irish President, Eamon de Valera (on left).

Shoebreakers Rosern

The Great Famine was central to the making of modern Ireland. Many important social changes had begun in the decades before 1845, but the Famine molded existing historical forces and gave them new meaning. Post-Famine Ireland was unique in 19th-century Europe. No other country shared its exceptional demography, was marked by such a lingering psychological trauma, or was so intimately connected with its overseas diaspora.

CHAPTER VII

EPILOGUE: THE LEGACY OF THE FAMINE

Post-Famine Ireland was a society of contrasts. Farmers with larger holdings acquired more land and became wealthier (right), but others, such as these stonebreakers photographed at Roscrea, County Tipperary, in 1853 (opposite), remained insecure and impoverished.

Economic Recovery

For landowners and larger farmers the post-Famine decades were years of steady improvement and prosperity. Clearance and consolidation had given proprietors a free hand in reorganizing their estates, and most sought to take advantage of the larger profits now to be made from pastoral agriculture.

The face of the landscape had changed, particularly in areas of better soil: By 1861 two-fifths of Irish land was grazing farms of one hundred acres or more. Commercial innovations accompanied the growth of the livestock export trade and an urban professional and mercantile middle class emerged to service it.

Not All Those Who Survived the Famine Gained from This Mid-Victorian Boom

The increases in living standards were not evenly distributed. Many of the dispossessed took to the road as itinerants or "travelers" and subsisted on the margins of Irish life. Decreased competition for work lessened the grinding poverty of the laborers, but on the western seaboard the old patterns of smallholding and potato-subsistence persisted, and communities still depended on seasonal migrant labor and money from abroad.

In 1852 the potato plant was healthy in most places, but the high yields of the pre-Famine period never returned. The blight reappeared in 1860–2, 1879, 1890, 1894, and 1897. Despite the alarm these failures caused, they did not lead to full-scale famines for several reasons: decreased dependency on the potato, the availability of alternative foods, and more generous spending by government and private charities. By the 1880s the stubborn political economy of the 1840s had been abandoned, and the British government was anxious to deny nationalist claims that it was indifferent to Irish distress. Below: Relief road works in County Donegal in the 1880s.

On the better land in the west the existence of cattle-raising "ranches" and sheep-runs, sometimes managed by English or Scottish farmers, focused resentment and kept the memory of Famine injustice fresh. Moreover, in much of Ireland, the retention of post-Famine gains was dependent on the maintenance of rigid social discipline.

Farmers now tended to pass their property on to a single heir. This entailed later, and usually arranged, marriages for the eldest sons, and the choice of emigration or a celibate life for those younger siblings who stayed on as farmworkers and housekeepers.

The economic impact of the Famine was complex, but without the blight the demand for labor would probably have increased, as rising livestock prices would have stimulated intensive potato production for animal feed. Instead, the loss of both the potato and over 200,000 smallholding families led to sharp falls in crop output and pushed agriculture into a cycle that enriched a few, while requiring large numbers to emigrate.

The main losers of the Famine were the cottiers and conacre laborers, who bore the brunt of starvation, eviction, and emigration. Except for the large graziers, Irish farmers also suffered during the Famine. Those who survived saw some rise in living standards in the 1850s, and they became the dominant group in Irish society in terms of numbers. Yet their gains should not be exaggerated; the pastoral economy was capital-intensive and regionally specialized and the lion's share of the profits went to landowners, large farmers, and merchants of the east. The landlord class, now shorn of its weaker members, emerged stronger in the 1850s. Above: A landlord receives a deputation of tenants.

These photographs from west County Donegal, taken in the 1870s, depict cabins relatively little altered from those described by Lord George Hill in 1838: "Each consists of four walls, built of large rough stones (sometimes they are merely sods), put together without mortar; no chimney, a front and back door…a small aperture in the wall, to be called, in courtesy, a window, but having no glass in it, a dried sheep skin being its substitute. One or two wooden stools, an iron potato-pot, sometimes an old crazy bedstead, filled up with heather or potatoes, and little or no bedclothes, with a churn, two or three piggins, a spade, a shovel, and a pipe, are the contents of the cabin, half of which …is given up to the cattle." While the western counties had been quiescent during the Great Famine, they became the focus for agrarian agitation and violence in the Land War of 1879–82, when potato failure and agricultural depression again raised the specter of starvation and mass eviction.

A Traumatized Society?

It is impossible to measure the psychological legacy of the Famine, but the decimation of the population undoubtedly left deep emotional scars. The impact and memory of the Famine varied geographically and socially: The east and north recovered rapidly, while memories lingered longest in the Irish-speaking districts of the west.

Literary sources and oral tradition suggest a changed atmosphere in the countryside. The cultural vitality of pre-Famine society was dimmed, traditional folk customs declined, and previously boisterous fairs became more orderly. Long-standing habits of hospitality appeared to be replaced by more commercial behavior. This transformation reflected not only the demographic dominance of the "strong" farmers with their values of respectability and "independence" but also the influence of Britain and America.

The Irish language was one of the foremost victims of the Famine. Use of English grew steadily in the 18th century, but in 1845 up to four million people still spoke Irish. Those who died or emigrated were disproportionately Irish-speaking and by 1851 the number of speakers had halved. The Famine reinforced the association between the Irish language and poverty or backwardness and accelerated its abandonment.

A "Devotional Revolution"

More formal observances and a decline in the magical aspects of religion were becoming universal by the 1850s. Such vernacular practices as "patterns" (the celebration of the feast days of Celtic saints) and seasonal rituals were disrupted and discredited by the Famine; the few that survived, like the Croagh Patrick pilgrimage, became more disciplined and orthodox.

Under the authoritarian and reformist leadership of Cardinal Paul Cullen, the Catholic Church emerged from the Famine as a powerful institution, playing an important political role.

As the population fell, the ratio of priests to people tripled between 1840 and 1900 and the total numbers of priests and members of religious orders soared. Both tended to be drawn from the ranks of the farming class, and they sympathized with its customs and aspirations.

The Protestant churches shared a similar moral puritanism and mutual sectarian hostility. Religious tensions were greatest in the thriving city of Belfast, which drew in the rural Protestant and Catholic poor.

The Resurgence of Nationalism

In the post-Famine political vacuum, landlords reasserted local control. Tenant associations set up to defend the social position of farmers proved unable to sustain themselves politically at a national level. Ireland displayed little of the populist political vitality that had characterized the O'Connell decades.

Yet the revolutionary tradition endured among many of the Famine survivors and reemerged as Fenianism. In America and Britain this was primarily an expression of

While popular recollections of the Famine were bitter, they were very often also tinged with shame. Survivors were reluctant to recall or pass on to their children personal experiences of suffering and poverty. Indeed, a folklore recorder in the 1940s noted "a sort of conspiracy of silence… about it all." The memories that were preserved tended to be pious, impersonal, or directed against such local targets as landlords or officials. Above: An open-air mass, County Donegal, in the 1860s.

Irish ethnic feeling, but in Ireland the hostility of the Church meant most farmers kept their distance.

An attempted Fenian rising in 1867 was a fiasco. Ironically, the movement's greatest success came later, as popular sympathy gathered behind the campaign to free interned prisoners. Even many of the clergy expressed anger at the execution of the three "Manchester martyrs" for accidentally killing a policeman during a rescue attempt. Such expressions of support for those who had suffered in the nationalist cause became a recurrent theme in post-Famine Irish politics.

The Land War

Potato failure in Connacht in 1879, following the onset of agricultural recession, raised the threat of renewed famine. With Fenian support, the Land League emerged as a national alliance of the farming and laboring classes. The inspired leadership of Charles Stewart Parnell held this disparate organization together.

The Fenian movement embraced both the secretive Irish Republican Brotherhood (IRB) in Ireland and fraternal societies in America, Britain, and Australia. Fenianism was always a minority element within Irish nationalism, but it gained wider sympathy following British repression in 1867 and again after the IRB-led Easter Rebellion of 1916. Above: James Stephens, the first Fenian leader, addresses a demonstration in America in 1864.

The long-simmering antagonism of landlords and tenants boiled over into an open "Land War" in 1879. Even the better-off tenants of the duke of Leinster in Kildare symbolically burned their leases in defiance (left). Michael Davitt, himself the son of a small farmer evicted from Mayo in 1850, voiced the radical demand for the abolition of landlordism and the redistribution of the land, but the "strong" farmers in the movement were prepared to settle for less. Prime Minister W. E. Gladstone's 1881 Land Act, which his critics alleged was extracted by Land League violence (below), granted official rent reductions and recognized the tenant's "interest" in his farm. This act satisfied most farmers outside the west. In 1882 Charles Stewart Parnell agreed to end the agitation in return for the government wiping out rent arrears.

As evictions rose in 1880–1, the League organized the obstruction of evictions and the "boycotting" of landlords and their allies. Parnell's political and social vision was markedly different from that of the revolutionaries, but his great skill lay in his ability to attune his rhetoric to his audience, while being politically pragmatic. Conscious of the power of popular memory, he repeatedly advocated "undoing the work of the Famine" as the ultimate aim of the League.

The Land War ended in 1882 with a profound defeat for landlords, who had to accept "dual ownership" with tenants. Land purchase acts in 1885 and 1903 rationalized the situation by offering loans to tenants to buy their farms. Yet little was achieved by the smallholders and laborers whose more radical expectations had been raised, only to be dashed. Although most Irish farmers owned their land by the 1920s, the work of the Famine was never really undone.

Contemporary Ireland and the Famine

The meaning of the Famine to modern
Ireland is complex and changing. To some,
particularly Republicans in the polarized
context of Northern Ireland, the Famine
continues to represent what it did to
historian John Mitchel—the ultimate case
of British oppression of the Irish people.

In the Irish Republic, which has, since
the 1960s, been opened up to modernizing
forces, the picture has become blurred.
"Revisionist" historians, anxious to wean
the Irish public away from myths of the past, tended to
play down the importance of the Famine or suggested
that it was somehow inevitable. Since the 1980s this view
has in turn been challenged by more serious studies of
the catastrophe, which have endorsed neither the wilder
claims of the Mitchelite tradition nor the complacent
platitudes that succeeded them.

The idea of famine runs deep in the Irish psyche, and
public recognition of the event—especially surrounding
its 150th anniversary in 1995—has, for the most part,
encouraged imaginative and positive expressions of
this. One excellent example is the Famine Museum at
Strokestown, County Roscommon, which opened in
1994. Here the outbuildings of an Anglo-Irish "big

This Irish cartoon from
1885 depicts "Famine"
alongside "Eviction" (a
landlord) and "Coercion"
(a policeman). To the
revolutionary generation
who created the inde-
pendent state of Ireland
between 1916 and 1922,
the Great Famine was
unquestionably a
British crime.

house" have been redesigned to display a selection of images, text, and documents explaining the catastrophe in its context. Illustrations of modern famines draw attention to the continuing fact of mass hunger and remind modern visitors of the ugly and horrifying realities of famine, past and present.

Ireland has become distinguished for the work of its international aid agencies, and in proportion to their means the Irish contribute more to "Third World" development than other European nations. Agencies such as AfrI, Concern, and Trócaire have stressed historical parallels between 1840s Ireland and modern developing countries, and are committed to internationalizing the memory of the Famine and confronting the ideologies that make such disasters possible.

The Famine became central to nationalist thinking with the publication in 1860 of John Mitchel's *The Last Conquest of Ireland (Perhaps)*. Mitchel blamed Irish depopulation on deliberate British policy. His vivid but one-dimensional interpretation endured because it served the deep psychological and political needs of the post-Famine generations.

Below: The Famine Museum in Strokestown, County Roscommon. Overleaf: The monument to the Famine in Dublin.

DOCUMENTS

The Traveler in Pre-Famine Ireland

British and other European travelers in pre-Famine Ireland were generally shocked by the poverty of the country and its people. Their comments reflected their assumptions about the roots of Irish social malaise.

Women selling poultry at Dungarvan market, 1830s.

The English agriculturist and writer Arthur Young gave an account of County Westmeath.

In conversation with Lord Longford I made many enquiries concerning the state of the lower classes, and found that in some respects they were in good circumstances, in others indifferent; they have, generally speaking, such plenty of potatoes, as always to command a bellyful; they have flax enough for all their linen, most of them have a cow and some two, and spin wool enough for their cloaths; all a pig, and numbers of poultry, and in general the complete family of cows, calves, hogs, poultry, and children, pig together in the cabbin; fuel they have in the utmost plenty; great numbers of families are also supported by the neighbouring lakes; which abound prodigiously with fish....

Reverse the medal: they are ill cloathed, and make a wretched appearance, and what is worse, are much oppressed by many who make them pay too dear for keeping a cow, horse, &c. They have a practice also of keeping accounts with the labourers, contriving by that means, to let the poor wretches have very little cash for their year's work. This is a great oppression, farmers and gentlemen keeping accounts with the poor is a cruel abuse....

Arthur Young
A Tour in Ireland 1776–1779, 1780

Chevalier de La Tocnaye, an émigré French nobleman, on "Whiteboyism"— or social agitation—in County Wexford.

In the month of July 1793 the White Boys experienced here a complete defeat, and since that time they have not shown themselves. As a great deal has been said and written about them, I believe it will be of interest if I give a few details about their existence. In every country of the world the peasant pays tithe with reluctance; everywhere it is regarded as an onerous impost, prejudicial to the spread of cultivation, for the labourer is obliged to pay on the product of his industry. In Ireland it seems to me a more vexatious tax than elsewhere, for the great mass of the people being Catholic, it seems to them hard that they should be obliged to maintain a minister who is often the only Protestant in the parish, and who exacts his dues with rigour. Beyond the ordinary tithe he has a right, over nearly the whole of Ireland, to one-tenth of the milk of a cow, one-tenth of the eggs, and one-tenth of the vegetables of the gardens. One can easily understand that these conditions may be very severe when the minister exacts his dues in kind, and especially when…these poor miserable folk have, as well, to supply a subsistence for their own priests. They have often made complaints and claims in connection with this subject, and to these it was hardly possible to give attention without overturning the whole of the laws of the Establishment, as it is called; that is to say, the Established religion. From complaints and claims the peasants come to threats, and from threats to the execution of the things threatened. They assembled at night in great numbers in certain parts of Ireland, and in order that they might recognise each other safely, they wore their shirts outside their clothes, from whence came the name of White Boys. In this garb they overran the country, breaking the doors and gates of ministers' houses, and if they could catch the cattle they mutilated them by cutting off their tails and ears. All the time they did no other violent act, and

a traveller might have gone through the country with perfect security. For different offences of the kind indicated the magistrates of Wexford arrested a score or so of the culprits, and immured them in the town prison. Their comrades demanded their liberation, and were not able to obtain it. They threatened then to come and free them by force, and advanced on the town to the number of two or three thousand.…

The Major in charge imprudently advanced before his soldiers in order to speak with the White Boys, and after some lively discussions, he received a blow from a scythe which laid him dead. Immediately on seeing this the soldiers fired, and in two or three minutes the whole force of the White Boys was broken up and put to flight, leaving behind them several hundreds dead. A few of the unfortunates who were wounded, fearing the punishment which would follow if they should be taken, dragged themselves as well as they could into the corn-fields and hedges, and there perished miserably.

After this battle nothing has been heard of the rebellious peasants, and the country has been quiet. This revolt seems to me to be in little, a perfect parallel to the Revolution in France in its beginnings.

Chevalier de La Tocnaye
*A Frenchman's Walk
through Ireland, 1796–7*
Translated and edited by
J. Stevenson, 1917

John Carr, an English travel writer, published this patronizing account of Irish potato dependency in 1806.

An Irish cabin, in general, is like a little antediluvian ark; for husband, wife and children, cow and calf, pigs, poultry, dog, and frequently cat, repose under the same roof in perfect amity. A whimsical calculation sometime since ascertained that in eighty-seven cabins there were one hundred and twenty full grown pigs, and forty-seven dogs. The rent of cabin and potatoe plot in the county of Wicklow and neighbourhood, is from one to two guineas; the family live upon potatoes and butter-milk six days in the week, and instead of "an added pudding," the Sabbath is generally celebrated by bacon and greens. … The price of labour was sixpence halfpenny per day.

Insufficiency of provision, which operates so powerfully against marriage in England, is not known or cared about in Ireland; there the want of an establishment never affects the brain of the enamoured rustic. Love lingers only until he can find out a dry bank, pick a few sticks, collect some furze and fern, knead a little mud with straw, and raise a hut about six feet high, with a door to let in the light and let out the smoke; these accomplished, the happy pair, united by their priest, enter their sylvan dwelling, and a rapid race of chubby boys and girls soon proves by what scanty means life can be sustained and imparted.

Upon an average, a man, his wife, and four children, will eat thirty-seven pounds of potatoes a day. A whimsical anecdote is related of an Irish potato. An Englishman, seeing a number of fine florid children in a cabin, said to the father: "How do your countrymen contrive to have so many fine children?" "*By Jasus it is the potatoe, Sir,*" said he.

Three pounds of good mealy potatoes are more than equivalent to one pound of bread. It is worthy of remark to those who live well, without reflecting upon the condition of others to whom

Interior of a small farmer's cabin, 1846. Potatoes are stored on a loft above the hearth to allow them to dry.

Providence has been less bountiful, that one individual who subsists upon meat and bread, consumes what would maintain five persons who live on bread alone, and twelve who subsist on potatoes….

When they dig out the potatoes in the autumn, they sow the ridge, immediately before digging, with bere [barley], and shelter the crop in a pit, piled up so as to form a sloping roof. Potatoes are said to be very propitious to fecundity; and I have been told that some investigators of political economy, enamoured with the fructifying qualities of the precious vegetable, have clothed it with political consequence; and in Ireland have regarded it like Cadmus's teeth, as the prime source of population; so that hereafter, the given number of potatoes necessary to the due proportion of vital fluid being found, it will only be necessary to have due returns of the potato crops, in order to ascertain the average number of little girls and boys, which have for the last year increased the circle of society…. I am ready to acknowledge the nutritious quality of the potatoe, and that it may be sufficient for the purposes of mere existence with an Irish rustic, who having little to do, does little: but an enlightened and experienced medical friend of mine assured me, that it could not supply the frame with its necessary support under the pressure of violent exercise. A workman in an ironfoundry would not be able to endure the fatigue of his duty for three hours together, if he had no other food than potatoes.

John Carr
The Stranger in Ireland: or, A Tour in the Southern and Western Parts of that Country in the Year 1805
1806

Henry Inglis, a Scottish travel writer, described the decline of Irish domestic industry.

Westport was once a very flourishing town. The linen trade was extensively carried on there; and eight years ago, as many as nine hundred pieces were measured and sold on a market day. Now the quantity scarcely averages one hundred pieces…. The linen trade in this district…is the source of all the extras which are obtained beyond the absolute necessaries of life. The land is let in very small portions; seven or eight acres is about the usual size of a "take." Potatoes are raised for the family consumption; grain, to pay the rent; and the flax is destined for clothing and extras. The decline of the linen trade has produced great want of employment; and the condition of the agricultural lists throughout these districts has very much deteriorated….

We have certainly no proof of a want of will among the Irish peasantry to work, in the thousands who travel every season from the remotest parts of Ireland, to earn a pound or two at laborious harvest work; and who carry back, sewed up in the sleeve of their ragged coat…these hard and far-sought earnings, to pay the rent for their cabin, and a bit of potato land.

Henry Inglis
A Journey throughout Ireland, 1835

The French writer Alexis de Tocqueville visited Newport, County Mayo.

In the newspapers we saw an article by a Mr. Hughes, parish priest of Newport Pratt, revealing that the people of his parish were starving and asking for help. We thought that we should go there to see Ireland in all its wretchedness….

We were surprised at seeing the village street and the quay filled with a great crowd of men, women and children. Some are seated on the bare ground, the rest are in a group. Our arrival generates a great sensation. We are surprised. They look at us with an avidity that we cannot understand. We leave our carriage and walk for some time in the street. More than a hundred persons follow us, without any demonstration but with a singular tenacity. Two or three speak to us; we understand that they took us to be government agents sent to relieve the distress.… The priest sees us and asks us to come in. A man of about fifty. An open and energetic face. A little stout. Strong accent. A little common. Dressed in black with riding boots.… We tell the priest that we read his letters in the newspapers, that we could not believe the extent of the evils of which he speaks, and that we came expressly to assure ourselves of the reality. He seems pleased that such is our intention. He tells us that he will allow us to leave only when we should be assured that he told the truth and invites us to dinner. During this time the whole crowd that we had seen in the street, knowing of the priest's return, was gathered in front of his door. We asked him what the crowd meant; he replies: I succeeded by means of the publications you have seen in collecting about 300 pounds sterling. I have received just now 40 more, he added, drawing them out of his pocket with an air of triumph and extreme satisfaction; I have organized a committee, three Catholics, three Protestants, to distribute this money under my supervision. We have bought oatmeal with this money; it arrived here two days ago, [and] I have put it in the shop that you see over there. The problem now is how we shall distribute

it. All these people that you see, he said, pointing to the crowd, are here in the hope of participating in this distribution.

We: But are all these people in need of help.

The priest: Most of them have not eaten since yesterday. Since this morning they are waiting there fasting. These men are small farmers paying a rent. The potato harvest partially failed last year, the scarcity since last March has begun to make itself felt. Those who had cows, sheep, and pigs have sold them in order to live. All those you see there have nothing more. For we give help only to those who no longer can sell anything to help themselves. For several months these unfortunates whom you see have been constantly therefore on the point of starving. They never eat their fill. Most of them have been forced to dig up the new harvest and feed themselves on potatoes as large as nuts, which make them ill.

At this moment, the priest opened the window facing the crowd. All the spectators immediately fell into a profound silence. The cry "*hear hear*" passed from mouth to mouth, and the priest, placed as in a pulpit, spoke roughly in these terms partly in English, partly in Irish:

I want you to know that our flour has finally arrived, but several members of the committee think that it would be better to try to sell a part of it. Mark, that it is a question of a sale at half price. I also think that it would be desirable that it be done so. Consider it well, and if you have some resources, bring us your money. The flour will be sold at half price and with what we will get, we will buy more. It is therefore in your interest to make, if it is possible, the effort we are asking of you. You see that we will not let those starve who absolutely cannot do what I advise. I have some bad news to tell you; the absence of several members of the committee, and the lack of time to make a correct list of the most necessitous among you, will prevent us from making the distribution this evening. Arm yourselves with patience. Those of you who still have some provisions, I say to you in the name of God, share them this evening with your neighbours and friends. Tomorrow help will come. He who would let his neighbour die for the deed of not giving him a potato, he is a murderer. Disperse. Go home. May God bless you....

This speech was made in a loud and animated voice. One saw in the face when he spoke the passionate interest that he had for the people, but at the same time an air of firmness and command. There was more kindness than gentleness in his voice. The crowd listened to him in silence. All eyes were fixed on him. Mouths were hanging open. The pale cheeks and the tired appearance of these unfortunates showed their suffering. From time to time one of the spectators made an observation in a loud voice. The priest argued with him a moment and then took up his discourse again. When he had finished speaking, a part of the crowd returned in silence, with resignation and order. The rest sat down again at the door and seemed to hope that in spite of his words, the priest would not be able to refrain from giving some help that evening.

After dinner we wanted to go out.... From the top of his steps, the priest spoke again to his people. He said that he could not help them all, and that he did not wish to choose between them. Your misery, he added, will have an end because it will become known. Here are, he said, pointing to us, two strangers who have come to this country only to learn the extent of your sufferings and make them known in their country; God bless them, shouted the crowd. They are our brothers, said the priest, they are Catholics like us. I hope, he added, fixing his eyes on some Protestants who were in the crowd, that there is in this language nothing that wounds you. You know that when it is a question of charity, I make no difference between Catholic and Protestant....

We passed through the crowd, which respectfully opened a path for us. In spite of all his efforts, the priest, who seemed very troubled, was not able to prevent himself from being concerned by the sight of some more wretched than others. I saw him slip a few small coins into some hands....

We: But all these parishes belong to a small number of landlords, the marquis of Sligo, Sir [R.] O'Donnel.... These men participate undoubtedly in works of charity during these times of distress.

The three priests, hotly and bitterly: It is an error, Sirs, these great landlords give nothing, do nothing, to prevent this unfortunate population from dying of hunger. It is the poor who support the poor.

We: But what is the cause of this?

The priest: There are several causes; almost all the great landlords are very embarrassed. Moreover, there is a profound hatred between them and the population. All the great families of this country are Catholics who have become Protestants to keep their property, or Protestants who have seized the property of Catholics. The population regards them as apostates or as conquerors and detests them. In return they do not feel any sympathy for them. They let farmers die before their eyes or evict them from their miserable dwellings on the slightest pretext.

We: The resignation of the people seems very great?

The priest: It is in fact. You have just seen two hundred unfortunates who are in real danger of starving to death and who can barely keep alive. Well, on the surrounding grasslands the marquis of Sligo has a thousand sheep; and several of his granaries are full. The population has no idea of seizing these means of subsistence. They would sooner die than touch them.

We: That shows admirable virtue.

The priest: You must not have any illusions, Sirs. Religion doubtless counts for much in this patience; but fear counts for even more. This unfortunate population has been so long a butt for so cruel a tyranny, it has been so decimated by the gibbet and transportation, that all energy has finally left them. They submit themselves to death sooner than resist. There is not a population on the continent that in the face of such miseries would not have its *Three Days* [French revolution, 1830]. And I confess that if I were in their position, and if I were not restrained by the strongest religious passions, I would indeed have difficulty in not revolting against this tyranny and unresponsive aristocracy.

These last words were spoken with a singular bitterness and were heartily echoed by the two other priests present. It was evident that these men, if they were not encouraging the people to revolt, would not be in the least sorry if they did revolt, and their indignation against the upper classes was lively and deep.

Alexis de Tocqueville's Journey in Ireland: July–August, 1835
Translated and edited by Emmet Larkin, 1990

The French sociologist Gustave de Beaumont, who had traveled with de Tocqueville in Newport, wrote on the state of the Irish poor.

I have seen the Indian in his forests, and the negro in his chains, and thought, as I contemplated their pitiable condition, that I saw the very extreme of human wretchedness; but I did not then know the condition of unfortunate Ireland. Like the Indian, the Irishman is poor and naked; but he lives in the midst of a society where luxury is eagerly sought, and where wealth is honoured. Like the Indian, he is destitute of the physical comforts which human industry and the commerce of nations procure; but he sees a part of his fellows enjoying the comforts to which he cannot aspire. In the midst of his greatest distress, the Indian preserves a certain independence, which has its dignity and its charms. Though indigent and famished, he is still free in his deserts, and the sense of this liberty alleviates many of his sufferings: the Irishman undergoes the same destitution without possessing the same liberty; he is subject to rules and restrictions of every sort: he is dying of hunger, and restrained by law; a sad condition, which unites all the vices of civilization to all those of savage life. Without doubt, the Irishman who is about to break his chains, and has faith in futurity, is not quite so much to be bewailed as the Indian or the slave. Still, at the present day, he has neither the liberty of the savage, nor the bread of servitude.

I will not undertake to describe all the circumstances and all the phases of Irish misery; from the condition of the small farmer, who starves himself that his children may have something to eat, down to the labourer, who, less miserable but more degraded, has recourse to mendicancy—from resigned indigence, which is silent in the midst of its sufferings, and sacrifices to that which revolts, and in its violence proceeds to crime.

Irish poverty has a special and exceptional character, which renders its definition difficult, because it can be compared with no other indigence. Irish misery forms a type by itself, of which neither the model nor the imitation can be found anywhere else.

In all countries, more or less, paupers may be discovered; but an entire nation of paupers is what was never seen until it was shown in Ireland. To explain the social condition of such a country, it would be only necessary to recount its miseries and its sufferings; the history of the poor is the history of Ireland.

Gustave de Beaumont
Ireland: Social, Political and Religious
Translated by W. C. Taylor
1839

The English novelist William Makepeace Thackeray visited Skibbereen.

Before you enter the city of Skibbereen, the tall new Poor-house presents itself to the eye of the traveller; of the common model, being a bastard-Gothic edifice, with a profusion...of cottage-ornée roofs, and pinnacles, and insolent looking stacks of chimneys. It is built for 900 people, but as yet not more than 400 have been induced to live in it, the beggars preferring the freedom of their precarious trade to the dismal certainty within its walls. Next we come to the chapel, a very large respectable-looking building of dark-grey stone; and presently, behold, by the crowd of blackguards in waiting, the "Skibbereen Perseverance" has found its goal, and you are inducted to the "Hotel" opposite....

As it was Sunday...the people came flocking into the place by hundreds, and you saw their blue cloaks dotting the road and the bare open plains beyond. The men came with shoes and stockings to-day, the women all bare-legged, and many of them might be seen washing their feet in the stream, before they went up into the chapel. The street seemed to be lined on either side with blue cloaks, squatting along the doorways as is their wont. Among these, numberless cows were walking too and fro, and pails of milk passing, and here and there a hound or two went stalking about....

You pass by one of the cabin-streets out of the town, into a country which for a mile is rich with grain, though bare of trees, then through a boggy, bleak district, from which you enter into a sort of sea of rocks, with patches of herbage here and there.... There was only one wretched village along the road, but no lack of population; ragged people who issued from their cabins as the coach passed, or were sitting by the way-side. Everybody seems sitting by the way-side here: one never sees this general repose in England—a sort of ragged lazy contentment.... These were very different cottages to those neat ones I had seen in Kildare. The wretchedness of them is quite painful to look at; many of the potato-gardens were half dug up, and it is only the first week in August, near three months before the potato is ripe and at full growth; and the winter still six months away.

William Makepeace Thackeray
The Irish Sketchbook
1843

Eyewitness to the Famine

A number of eyewitness accounts were published during the Famine. Most were written by philanthropists who wanted to reveal the shocking realities of Irish suffering.

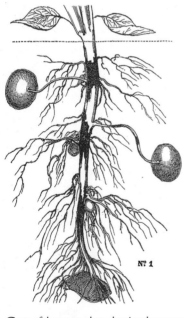

S tem of the potato plant, showing the ravages of the blight.

W. Steuart Trench was an Irish land agent and experimental farmer in Queen's County (Laois) at the beginning of the Famine period. This is his account of the second attack of the potato blight.

On August 1st of that calamitous year, 1846, I was startled by hearing a sudden and strange rumour that all the potato fields in the district were blighted; and that a stench had arisen emanating from their decaying stalks. I immediately rode up to visit my crop, and test the truth of this report; but I found it as luxuriant as ever, in full blossom, the stalks matted across each other with richness, and promising a splendid produce, without any unpleasant smell whatever. On coming down from the mountain, I rode into the lowland country, and there I found the report to be but too true. The leaves of the potatoes on many fields I passed were quite withered, and a strange stench, such as I had never smelt before, but which became a well-known feature in "the blight" for years after, filled the atmosphere adjoining each field of potatoes.

The next day I made further inquiries, and I found the disease was fast extending, and on rooting up some of the potato bulbs under the withered stalks, I found that decay had set in, and that the potato was rapidly blackening and melting away. In fields having a luxuriant crop, the stench was generally the first indication of disease, and the withered leaf followed in a day or two afterwards. Much alarm now prevailed in the country; people looked blank enough, as they asked each other if they had seen this new and formidable disease. Those, like me, who had staked a large amount of capital on the crop, hitherto almost a certainty, and at least as sure as the crop of wheat or turnips or any other agricultural produce, became extremely uneasy; whilst the poorer farmers looked on helplessly and with feelings of dire dismay at the total disappearance of all they had counted on for food....

On August 6, 1846—I shall not readily forget the day—I rode up as usual to my mountain property, and my feelings may be imagined when before I saw the crop, I smelt the fearful stench, now so well known and recognized as the death-sign of each field of potatoes...the luxuriant stalks soon withered, the leaves decayed, the disease extended to the tubers, and the stench from the rotting of such an immense amount of rich vegetable matter became almost intolerable....

But my own losses and disappointments, deeply as I felt them, were soon merged in the general desolation, misery, and starvation which now rapidly affected the poorer classes around me and throughout Ireland. It is true that in the more cultivated districts of the Queen's County and the midland counties generally, not many deaths occurred from actual starvation. I mean, that people were not found dead on the roads or in the fields from sudden deprivation of food; but they sank gradually from impure and insufficient diet; and fever, dysentery, the crowding in the workhouse or hardship on the relief works, carried thousands to a premature grave. The crop of all crops, on which they depended for food, had suddenly melted away, and no adequate arrangements had been made to meet this calamity,—the extent of which was so sudden and so terrible that no one had appreciated it in time—and thus thousands perished almost without an effort to save themselves.

W. Steuart Trench
Realities of Irish Life, 1868

The American pacifist Elihu Burritt visited Skibbereen in February 1847.

Among the attenuated apparitions of humanity that thronged this gate of stinted charity, one poor man presented himself under circumstances that even distinguished his case from the rest. He lived several miles from the centre of the town, in one of the rural districts, where he found himself on the eve of perishing with his family of seven small children. Life was worth the last struggle of nature, and the miserable skeleton of a father had fastened his youngest child to his back, and with four more by his side, had staggered up to the door.... The hair upon his face was nearly as long as that upon his head. His cheeks were fallen in, and his jaws so distended that he could scarcely articulate a word.... [The children's] appearance, though common to thousands of the same age in this region of the shadow of death, was indescribable. Their paleness was not that of common sickness. There was no sallow tinge in it. They did not look as if newly raised from the grave and to life before the blood had begun to fill their veins anew; but as if they had just been thawed out of the ice, in which they had been imbedded until their blood had turned to water.

Elihu Burritt
A Journal of a Visit of Three Days to Skibbereen, and its Neighbourhood
1847

William Bennett, an English Quaker, visited Erris, County Mayo, to distribute seed in March 1847. Here he describes the inhabitants of cabins at Belmullet.

[L]anguage utterly fails me in attempting to depict the state of the wretched inmates. I would not willingly add another to the harrowing details that have been told; but still they are the FACTS of actual experience; for the knowledge of which we stand accountable. I have certainly sought out one of the most remote and destitute corners; but still it is within the bounds of our Christian land, under our Christian Government, and entailing upon us—both as individuals and as members of a human community —a Christian responsibility from which no one of us can escape. My hand trembles while I write. The scenes of human misery and degradation we witnessed will haunt my imagination, with the vividness and power of some horrid and tyrannous delusion, rather than the features of a sober reality. We entered a cabin. Stretched in one dark corner, scarcely visible, from the smoke and rags that covered them, were three children huddled together. Lying there *because they were too weak to rise,* pale and ghastly, their little limbs—on removing a portion of the filthy covering—perfectly emaciated, eyes sunk, voice gone, and evidently in the last stage of actual starvation. Crouched over the turf embers was another form, wild and all but naked, scarcely human in appearance. It stirred not, nor noticed us. On some straw, soddened upon the ground, moaning piteously, was a shrivelled old woman, imploring us to give her something,—baring her limbs partly, to show how the skin hung loose from the bones, as soon as she attracted our attention. Above her, on something like a ledge, was a young woman, with sunken cheeks,— a mother I have no doubt,—who scarcely raised her eyes in answer to our enquiries, but pressed her hand upon her forehead, with a look of unutterable anguish and despair. Many cases were widows, whose husbands had recently been taken off by the fever, and thus their only pittance, obtained from the public works, entirely cut off. In many the husbands or sons were prostrate, under that horrid disease,— the results of long-continued famine and low living,—in which first the limbs, and then the body, swell most frightfully, and finally burst. We entered upward of fifty of these tenements. The scene was one and invariable, differing in little but the number of the sufferers, or of the groups, occupying the several corners within.… Perhaps the poor children presented the most piteous and heart-rending spectacle. Many were too weak to stand, their little limbs attenuated,—except when the frightful swellings had taken the place of previous emaciation,—beyond the *power of volition when moved.* Every infantile expression entirely departed; and in some, reason and intelligence had evidently flown. Many were *remnants of families,* crowded together in one cabin; orphaned little relatives taken in by the equally destitute, and even strangers, for these poor people are kind to one another to the end. In one cabin was a sister, just dying, lying by the side of her little brother, just dead. I have worse than this to relate, but it is useless to multiply details, and they are, in fact, unfit. They did but rarely complain. When inquired of, what was the matter, the answer was alike in all,—*"Tha shein ukrosh"—indeed the hunger.* We truly learned the terrible meaning of that sad word, *ukrosh.*

William Bennett
Narrative of a Recent Journey of Six Weeks in Ireland
1847

James Hack Tuke, a Quaker from York, condemned the mass evictions in Connacht.

The landlords of Mayo, as well as of many other portions of Connaught, as a class, (there are many noble exceptions who feel and see the impolicy and evil of such proceedings,) are pursuing a course which cannot fail to add to the universal wretchedness and poverty which exist. The corn crops, bountiful as they may be, are not sufficient to meet the landlords' claim for rent and arrears contracted during the last two years of famine, and it is at least not unnatural for the tenant to be unwilling to give up that, without which he must certainly perish. In every direction, the agents of the landlords, armed with the full powers of the law, are at work—everywhere one sees the driver or bailiff "canting" the small patches of oats or potatoes—or keepers, whose extortionate charges must be paid by the unfortunate tenant, placed over the crop. Even the produce of seed, distributed through the agency of benevolent associations, has been totally swept away. To add to the universal distress caused by this system of seizure, eviction is in many cases practised, and not a few of the roofless dwellings which meet the eye, have been destroyed at the instance of the landlords, after turning adrift the miserable inmates; and this even at a time like the present, when the charity of the whole world has been turned towards the relief of this starving peasantry. Whilst upon the island of Achill, I saw a memorable instance of this mode of proceeding, at the wretched fishing village of Kiel. Here, a few days previous to my visit, a driver of Sir R. O'Donnells, whose property it is, had ejected some twenty families, making, as I was informed, with a previous recent eviction, about forty. A crowd of these miserable ejected creatures collected around us, bewailing, with bitter lamentations, their hard fate. One old grey-headed man came tottering up to us, bearing in his arms his bed-ridden wife, and putting her down at our feet, pointed, in silent agony to her, and then to his roofless dwelling, the charred timbers of which were scattered in all directions around. This man said he owed little more than one year's rent, and had lived in the village, which had been the home of his forefathers, all his life. Another man, with five motherless children, had been expelled, and their "boiling-pot" sold for 3s. 6d. Another family, consisting of a widow and four young children, had their only earthly possession "a little sheep," seized, and sold for 5s. 6d.! But it is needless to multiply cases; instances sufficient have been given to show the hardships and misery inflicted. From this village alone, at least one hundred and fifty persons had been evicted, owing from half a year's to a year and a half's rent. The whole of their effects, even the miserable furniture of these wretched cabins seized and sold to satisfy the claims of the nominal owner of Achill.

What prospects are there for these miserable outcasts? Death indeed must be the portion of some, for their neighbours, hardly richer than themselves, were principally subsisting upon turnip tops; whilst the poor-house of the union of Westport is nearly forty miles distant. Turnips taken, can we say stolen, from the fields, as they wearily walked thither, would be their only chance of support.

A family evicted and a cottage knocked down, 1848.

Some indeed would never reach their destination—death would relieve them of their sufferings, and the landlord of his burden.

James Hack Tuke
A Visit to Connaught in the Autumn of 1847
1847

Asenath Nicholson was an American evangelical who had been in Ireland for three years when the Famine began. She visited Louisburgh, County Mayo, in spring 1848.

The little town of Louisburgh, two miles from "Old Head," had suffered extremely. An active priest and faithful protestant curate were doing to their utmost to mitigate the suffering, which was like throwing dust in the wind; *lost, lost* for ever—the work of death goes on, and what is repaired to-day is broken down to-morrow. Many have fallen under their labours. The graves of the protestant curate and his wife were pointed out to me in the church-yard, who had fallen since the famine, in the excess of their labour; and the present curate and his praiseworthy wife, unless they have supernatural strength, cannot long keep up the dreadful struggle....

The road [into the Killery mountains] was rough, and we constantly were meeting pale, meagre-looking men, who were on their way from the mountains to break stones, and pile them mountain-high, for the paltry compensation of a pound of meal a-day; these men had put all their seed into the ground, and if they gave up their cabins, they must leave the crop for the landlord to reap, while they must be in a poor-house or in the open air. This appeared to be the last bitter drug in Ireland's cup of woe! Why? a poor man was asked, whom we met dragging sea-weed to put upon his potato field, "do you do this, when you tell us you expect to go to the poor-house, and leave your crop to another?" "I will put it on, hoping that God Almighty will send me the work to get a bit."

We met flocks of wretched children going to school for the "bit of bread," some crying with hunger, and some begging to get in without the penny which was required for their tuition. The poor emaciated creatures went weeping away, one saying he had been "looking for a penny all day yesterday, and could not get it." The doctor who accompanied us returned to report to the priest the cruelty of the relieving-officer and the teacher, but this neither frightened or softened these hard hearts. These people are shut in by mountain and the sea on one side, and roads passable only on foot on the other, having no bridges, and the paths entirely lost in some places among the stones …though we met multitudes in the last stages of suffering, yet not one through that day asked charity, and in one case the common hospitality showed itself, by offering us milk when we asked for water. This day I saw enough, and my heart was sick—sick.

Asenath Nicholson
Lights and Shades of Ireland
1850

S. Godolphin Osborne was a Church of England clergyman with a record of

philanthropic journalism. Here he writes about the state of Limerick workhouse in summer 1850.

The first Union-house we visited was that at Limerick. Last year, when I went over it, I found it clean and in good order; I now found it every way the reverse. In the parent and auxiliary houses these was no less a number than 8000 paupers; every department, except the fever hospital, shewed evident symptoms of gross neglect. I have no words with which I can give any real idea of the sad condition of the inmates of two large yards at the parent house, in which were a very large number of young female children; many of them were clothed in the merest dirty rags, and of these they wore a very scanty allowance; they were in the dirt collected on their persons for many weeks; there was not about them the slightest evidence of any of the least care being taken of them; as they filed before me, two and two, they were a spectacle to fill any humane heart with indignation: sore feet, sore hands, sore heads; ophthalmia evident in the case of the great proportion of them; some of them were suffering from it in its very worst stage; they were evidently eat up with vermin—very many were mere skeletons: I know well what the appearance of a really famine-stricken child is; there were, it is true, some here who had brought their death-like appearance into the house with them; but the majority were as the type in which the one word *neglect* was printed, in no mistakable characters—the neglect of the latter state, not the consequence of the former state.

S. Godolphin Osborne
Gleanings in the West of Ireland
1850

Emigration

Victorian philanthropists were anxious to throw light on the hardships emigration entailed. Some even traveled with the Irish poor across the Atlantic in order to publicize their plight.

Robert Whyte, a middle-class emigrant, gives an account of a "coffin ship" crossing to Quebec in 1847.

June 15, 1847: The reports this morning were very afflicting, and I felt much that I was unable to render any assistance to my poor fellow passengers. The captain desired the Mistress to give them everything out of his own stores that she considered to be of service to any of them. He felt much alarmed; nor was it to be wondered at that contagious fever—which under the most advantageous circumstances and under the watchful eyes of the most skilful physicians requires the greatest ability —should terrify one having the charge of so many human beings, likely to fall prey to the unchecked progress of the dreadful disease. For once having shown

Irish emigrants on board a ship at Liverpool, 1846.

itself in the unventilated hold of a small brig, containing 110 living creatures, how could it possibly be stayed without suitable medicines, medical skill and pure water to slake the patients' burning thirst. The prospect before us was indeed an awful one, and there was no hope for us but in the mercy of God.

June 16: The past night was very rough, and I enjoyed little rest. No additional cases of sickness were reported, but there were signs of insubordination amongst the healthy men who complained of starvation and want of water for their sick wives and children. A deputation came aft to acquaint the captain with their grievances, but he ordered them away, and would not listen to a word from them. When he went below the ring leaders threatened that they would break into the provision store.... In order to make a deeper impression on their minds, he brought out the old blunderbuss from which he fired a shot, the report of which was equal to the report of a small cannon. The deputation slunk away muttering complaints. If they were resolute they could easily have seized upon the provisions. In fact, I was surprised how famished men could so easily bear with their own and their starved children's sufferings. The captain would willingly have listened if it were in his power to relieve their distress....

June 24: Being the festival of St John, and a Catholic holiday, some young men and women got up a dance in the evening, regardless of the moans and crys of those tortured by the fiery fever. When the mate spoke to them of the impropriety of such conduct they desisted and retired to the bow where they sat down and spent the remainder of the evening singing. The monotonous

Dancing between decks on an emigrant ship, 1850.

howling they kept up was quite in union with the scene of desolation within, and the dreary expanse of ocean without.

June 25: This morning there was a further accession to the names upon the sick roll. It was awful how suddenly some were stricken. A little child, playing with his companions, suddenly fell down, and for some time sunk in deadly torpor, from which when he awoke he commenced to scream violently and wreath in convulsive agony. A poor woman who was warming a drink at the fire for her husband also dropped down quite senseless and was borne to her berth. I found it very difficult to acquire precise information respecting the progressive symptoms of the disease, I inferred that the first symptom was generally a reeling in the head followed by a swelling pain, as if the head were going to burst. Next came excruciating pains in the bones, and then a swelling of the limbs, commencing with the feet, and in some cases ascending the body, and again descending before it reached the head, stopping at the throat. The period of this stage varied in different patients, some of them were covered in yellow, watery pimples, and the others with red and purple spots that turned into putrid sores.

June 27: It made my heart bleed to listen to the calls of "Water, for God's sake, water." Oh it was horrifying; strange to say I had no fear of taking the fever which, perhaps under the merciful providence of the Almighty, was a preventive cause....

July 28, Grosse Isle: By 6 AM we were settled in our new position before the quarantine station.... The poor passengers, expecting that they would be all reviewed, were dressed in their best clothes and were clean, though haggard and weak. They were greatly disappointed in their expectations as they were under the impression that the sick would be immediately admitted to the hospital and the healthy landed upon the island, there to remain until taken to Quebec by a steamer...I could not believe it possible that here, within reach of help, we should be left as neglected as when upon the ocean. That after a voyage of two months' duration we were to be left still enveloped by reeking pestilence, the sick without medicine, medical skill, nourishment or so much as a drop of pure water— for the river, although not saline here, was polluted by the most disgusting objects thrown overboard from the several vessels....

August 1: While the captain was away with the boat, the steamer came along-side of us to take our passengers. It did not take very long to transship them as few of them had any luggage. Many of them were sadly disappointed when they learned that they were to be carried on to Montreal, as those who had left their relatives upon Grosse Isle hoped that, as Quebec was not far distant, they would be enabled by some means to hear of them by staying there....

Of the passengers I never afterwards saw any but two, both of them young men who got employment upon the Lachine Canal. The rest wandered over the country, carrying nothing with them but disease, and that but few of them survived the severity of the succeeding winter (ruined as their constitutions were) I am quite confident.

Robert Whyte
The Ocean Plague: A Voyage to Quebec in an Irish Immigrant Vessel
1848

In this letter to Lord Hobart on the Committee of Colonization, Vere Foster, a British diplomat turned social reformer, described the appalling conditions aboard the specially built American emigrant vessel Washington *on the crossing from Liverpool to New York.*

17th November—The doctor this evening heaved overboard a great many of the chamber-pots belonging to the female passengers, saying that henceforward he would allow no women to do their business below, but that they should come to the filthy privies on deck. I heard him say, "There are a hundred cases of dysentery in the ship, which will all turn to cholera, and I swear to God that I will not go amongst them; if they want medicines they must come to me." This morning the first mate took it into his head to play the hose upon the passengers in occupation of the waterclosets, drenching them from head to foot; the fourth mate did the same a few mornings ago....

21st November—A violent gale commenced this evening.

22d—The gale became perfectly terrific; for a few minutes we all expected momentarily to go to the bottom, for the sea, which was foaming and rolling extremely high, burst upon

Irish emigrants in the steerage of a ship bound for America, 1850.

the deck with a great crash, which made us all believe that some part of the vessel was stove in. The wave rushed down into the lower deck, and I certainly expected every moment to go down. Some of the passengers set to praying; the wind blew a perfect hurricane, so that it was quite out of the question to attempt to proceed on our proper course. We therefore scudded before the wind, having the main-topsail close reefed and the fore-topsail staysail only. The water which had rushed upon the deck remained there to the depth of several feet; it was got rid of by breaking holes in the bulwarks with a hatchet. The whole sea was a sheet of foam. Towards 9 PM the gale began to be less, though still violent, and moderated during the night.

25th November—Another child, making about 12 in all, died of dysentery from want of proper nourishing food, and was thrown into the sea sown up, along with a great stone, in a cloth. No funeral service has yet been performed, the doctor informs me, over any one who has died on board; the Catholics objecting, as he says, to the performance of any such service by a layman. As there was no regular service, the man appointed to attend to the passengers seized the opportunity, when the sailors pulling at the rope raised the usual song of—

"Haul in the bowling, the Black Star
    bowling,
Haul in the bowling, the bowling
    haul—"

to throw in the child overboard at the sound of the last word of the song, making use of it as a funeral dirge....

3d December—A few of the passengers were taken ashore to the Hospital at Staten Island, and we arrived alongside the quay at New York this afternoon. The 900 passengers dispersed as usual among the various fleecing houses, to be partially or entirely disabled for pursuing their travels into the interior in search of employment.

Letter from Vere Foster
to Lord Hobart
1 December 1850

These letters from the medical superintendent at Grosse Isle and the emigration agent at Quebec describe conditions at the Grosse Isle Canada, quarantine station in 1847.

Every vessel bringing Irish passengers (but more especially those from Liverpool and Cork), has lost many by fever and dysentery on the voyage, and has arrived here with numbers of sick.… Seventeen vessels have [recently] arrived with Irish passengers; five from Cork, four from Liverpool, and the others from Sligo, Limerick, Belfast, Londonderry and New Ross. The number of passengers with which these vessels left port was 5607; out of these the large number of 260 died on the passage, and upwards of 700 have been admitted to hospital, or are being treated on board their vessels, waiting vacancies to be landed. The number now under treatment…is 695, and there remain on board the ships *Aberdeen* and *Achilles* from Liverpool, and the ship *Bee* from Cork, and *Wolfville* from Sligo, 164 sick, who receive medical assistance on board, and will be landed as accommodation can be made by turning passengers' sheds into hospitals.

I have taken upon me to engage the services of Drs. Jacques and McGrath …but shall require at least two more medical assistants, as these gentlemen have already charge of upwards of 300 sick, and will be unable to give attendance to the large number still to land, without taking into account the number who may arrive among the many thousands now due.

Letter from Dr. G. M. Douglas to H. Daly, Grosse Isle, 24 May 1847, Parliamentary Papers, House of Commons, 1847–8

Out of the 4000 or 5000 emigrants that have left [Grosse Isle] since Sunday, at least 2000 will fall sick somewhere before three weeks are over. They ought to have accommodation for 2000 sick at least in Montreal or Quebec, as all the Cork and Liverpool passengers are half dead from starvation and want before embarking; and the least bowel complaint, which is sure to come with change of food, finishes them without a struggle. I never saw people so indifferent to life; they would continue in the same berth with a dead person until the seamen or captain dragged out the corpse with boat-hooks. Good God! what evils will befall the cities wherever they alight. Hot weather will increase the evil.

Letter from A. C. Buchanan to Major Campbell, Quebec, 9 June 1847, Parliamentary Papers, House of Commons, 1847–8

The Canadian Parliament appealed to Britain to impose restrictions on emigration.

We, your Majesty's most dutiful and loyal subjects…humbly venture to represent the apprehensions which we entertain, from the unprecedented influx of emigrants from Great Britain and Ireland, in a state of destitution, starvation and disease, unparalleled in the history of the province.

We venture humbly to state, that the arrangements for the reception of the sick at Grosse Isle, the quarantine station, although made on an extensive scale, have proved wholly inadequate to the unexpected emergency; that the entire range of buildings intended for the use of emigrants generally, at the station, have been converted into hospitals, and are still insufficient for the numerous and increasing sick; but the island itself, which is three miles in length and a mile and a half in breadth, has been reported as not sufficiently extensive to receive all those who by the regulation of the health officers are required to perform quarantine; and that the apparently healthy have consequently been forwarded without being subjected to the usual precaution....

We feel bound to declare...that while we believe that this House and the people of the province are most desirous to welcome to the colony all those of their fellow-subjects who may think it proper to emigrate from the parent country to settle amongst them, we are convinced that a continued emigration of a similar character to that which is now taking place, is calculated to produce a most injurious effect upon our prosperity, unless conducted upon some more systematic principle.

We beseech the interference of your Majesty under the affliction with which this land has been visited, and is still further threatened, not to permit the helpless, the starving, the sick and diseased, unequal and unfit as they are to face the hardships of a settler's life, to embark for these shores, which if they reach, in too many instances only to find a grave.

We humbly pray your Majesty that measures may be adopted by your Majesty's Government, that emigrant ships may be large and airy, that ample space may be allotted to the emigrants, and that a larger allowance of better food than is now furnished, with sufficient medical attendance, shall be always provided on board....

Address from the Legislative Assembly of Canada, 25 June 1847, Parliamentary Papers, House of Commons, 1847–8

Some of the surviving emigrants wrote to their relatives in Ireland. The following collection of letters was submitted by Sir Robert Gore Booth to Parliament. It includes both the optimistic report of the ship captain whom Gore Booth employed to transport his tenants and the more mixed feelings of the County Sligo men and women whom he had deposited in New Brunswick in 1847.

Noble Sir, I am happy to inform you that I Got Clear of My passengers, in Souch a Manner as will giv you pleasure whin you hear all the particulars Connected with the Voyage. Sir Your Kind acts at hoam to privint famine and to Elivate the Condition of the Poor is as well nowen here as in the Town of Sligow[.] Your Ever Thankful Tennants were Highley Respected on being landed in this Town[.] [T]he Mayor Town Counsel &c. provided thim with large House attached to the Publick Buildings where the[y] were lodged and Kindley threated by the Community in General[,] Every one Vying how [they] could Show thim the most Kindness. I Sent them 28lbs [of] Meal flour Bread &c. to the lodgeing and will continue to furnish thim while I Remain in Port[.] [T]he[y] are Scattering fast[.] I got all the Girls Leady Booth gave in My Charge good and Respectable Mrs [mistresses] where the[y] will be Kindley threathed. [A]ll the Cabin Passengers are provided for, and the Rest are geting Good Employment Verry fast...the Health Officers Reaport to the Governor was that Sir Robert's Passengers or Tennants could not be classed as Common advintururs, or Emigrants, or his Brother's Ship Classed among the dirty old Emigrant hired Vessels, as the Cleaness of the Ship the Style of order Kept up the Health and Cleaness of the Passengers, the Good Diet, the Superior Medicine and the Supplying of Clean Bead Cloaths [and] The pure Ventilation all combined to Make her Superior to Any of her Magesty's Thransports....

Letter from Captain Michael Driscoll
of the ship *Æolus* to
Sir Robert Gore Booth
St. John, New Brunswick
13 June 1847

Dear mother and brother[,] I take the favourable oppurtunity of writting these few lines to you hoping to find you are all in as good health as this laves me and my sister at present thanks be to God for all his mercies to us[.] Dear mother[,] we were very uneasy for ever coming to this country for we were in a bad State of health[.] During The Voiage their was a very bad fever aboard[;] Pebby was taken to the Cabbin by the Captains wife and was there from a week we were on Sea till we come to quarentine and took the fever on the Ship[.] [T]hen all the passengers that did not pass the Doctor was sent to the Isleand and she was kept by the Captains wife then on laving the ship. Pebby was relapsed again and sent to Hospital and remained their nine or ten days but thanks be to God we got over all the Disorders belonging the Ship[.] I was at work at A Dollar per day But the place got very bad and no regard for new passengers [nor] even a nights Lodgeing could be easy found[.] I met with Andy Kerrigan and he took me with him to his house and remained their for amounth Boarding[.] Mary took a very Bad fever and was Despaired of Both by priest and Doctor And as soon as She got well Andy took the Same disease[.] I am

Sorry to relate that poor Biddy Clancy and Catherine McGowan Died in Hospital and A great many of our friends[.] [T]heir is Aprospect of the winter Been very bad and I offten wished to be at home again Bad and all as we were[.] [W]e offten wished we never Seen St John[.] Dear Mother[,] I hope you will Let me [k]now as soon as possible how are you all my Sisters and poor Brother and all in good health[.] [I]t is all we are Sorry for that we cannot Send any relief to you[,] But this place is Different to our opinions at home any new pasengers except the[y] have friends before them are in Distress[.] [I]ts very [hard] to get work here except them that are in Steady employment[.] The government are about to Send all the passengers that were Sent out here by Lord Pamistown [Palmerston] and Sir Robert Home again Because the[y] are sure that all of them that did not perish that the[y] surely will this winter[.] Dear mother[,] let us [k]now how ye are getting on or are you all in good health[.] I am very glad that Catherine did not come to this place for a great deal of our neighbours Died here.... Let us [k]now how does the markets Rate or is the publick works in force or any relief given Since we left.... A great many of the passengers went out to the country and could get no employ[.] Bad as the City is it is better than the Country....

Bryan Clancy and his sister
St. John, New Brunswick
17 November 1847

Dear Father & Mother. I take the present opportunity of letteng you know that I am in good health[,] hoping this will find you and all friends the same. I wrote you shortly after I came here but recevid no answer which make me very uneasy untill

I hear from you and how you are and all friends. Dear Father[,] we had a pretty favourable passage[;] we Cast Anchor at Partridge Island after 5 Weeks passage[.] [T]here were 4 Deaths on the passage but the Second day after we arrived here and after the Doctor came on Board the Sickness commenced[.] [W]e were then put on the Island for 3 Weeks and the end of which time my dear Litle Biddy died[.] [T]hank God I got safe off and continues to enjoy good health since[.] Dear Father[,] Pen could not write the distress of the Irish Passengers which arrived here thro Sickness death and distress of every Kind[.] [T]he Irish I know have suffered much and is still suffering but the Situation of them here even the Survivors at that awful time was lamentable in the extreme[.] [T]here are thousands of them buried in the Island and those who could not go to the States are in the Poorhouse or begging thro the streets of St John.... If you would wish to come here I would like you was here as I think times will mend here after some time and dear Father I will soon send you some help.... I went to the country with my uncle but he went off to the States since[.] [L]et uncle Paddy know that Thos. went to Boston with his uncle[.] Thos. got a place for the Boys in Boston.... No more at Present But [I] remains your affectionate Daughter till Death....

Catherine Hennagan
St. John, New Brunswick
15 February 1848

Dear Mother[,] I Rite these fue Lines to you hoping To find you in good health As this Leaves Me at preasant I thank god for it[.] Dear mother[,] we were Foure weeks at say and we got afone passage[.] God favoured me i never was one Day sick i thank god For it[.] [T]he

The lament of the Irish emigrant.

very Night that I landed i got sick and kept the Bed for two weekes and after that i fell in to good employment At four shilling per Day British Money[.] Dear Mother[,] my sister Elon was Imployed the Day after we Laned in St Jonhs New Brunswick[.] Dear Mother[,] the day we landed my Sister Marget left St Jonhs New Brunswick and went to Boston wich i was very sorry that i did not Get to see her[.] [M]y Sister Elon went after her To Boston and I got no Acount from them since I parted her[.] [I] am working At preasant in the State of Maine on Real Road the rate of wages all this Summer was four shilling per Day British[.] The wages Dureing the winter is three shilling per Day we have a great Dale of Broken time here frost and snow and wet weather. Dear Mother[,] i am getting along well here and getting good health i thank God for it...this is a good contry for strong Boded men and very good pleace for girls[.] [G]ood smart girls have 6s. shilling per week and their Board....

Direct your Letter to Agusta State of Maine One Boyle.

One [Eoin] Boyle
Augusta, Maine
13 December 1847

Interpretations

The Irish Famine called forth a range of responses. For "moralist" ministers and officials, it was the improvident behavior of the Irish people—landlord and laborer alike—that had induced God to send the blight. Irish writers attacked British parsimony or landlord heartlessness.

THE NEW IRISH STILL.
SHOWING HOW ALL SORTS OF GOOD THINGS MAY BE OBTAINED (BY INDUSTRY) OUT OF PEAT.

This 1849 caricature expresses the British delusion that only exertion was needed to lift Ireland out of famine.

In 1846 Charles Trevelyan distributed copies of British statesman Edmund Burke's pamphlet advocating reliance on laissez-faire during times of scarcity.

The balance between consumption and production makes price. The market settles, and alone can settle, that price. Market is the meeting and conference of the *consumer* and *producer,* when they mutually discover each other's wants. Nobody, I believe, has observed with any reflection what market is, without being astonished at the truth, the correctness, the celerity, the general equity, with which the balance of wants is settled. They who wish the destruction of that balance, and would fain by arbitrary regulation decree, that defective production should not be compensated by encreased price, directly lay their *axe* to the root of production itself....

I beseech the Government...seriously to consider that years of scarcity or plenty, do not come alternately or at short intervals, but in pretty long cycles and irregularly, and consequently that we cannot assure ourselves, if we take a wrong measure, from the temporary necessities of one season; but that the next, and probably more, will drive us to the continuance of it, so that in my opinion, there is no way of preventing this evil which goes to the destruction of all our agriculture, and of that part of our internal commerce which touches our agriculture the most nearly, as well as the safety and very being of Government, but manfully to resist the very first idea, speculative or practical, that it is within the competence of Government, taken as Government, or even of the rich, as rich, to supply to the poor, those necessaries which it has pleased the Divine Providence for a while to with-hold from them. We, the people, ought to be made sensible, that it is not in breaking the laws of commerce, which are the laws of nature, and consequently the laws of God, that we are to place our hope of softening the divine displeasure to remove any calamity under which we suffer, or which hangs over us.

Edmund Burke
Thoughts and Details on Scarcity, 1800

In late 1847 Charles Trevelyan composed an apologia defending the relief policy that had been implemented.

Ireland is not the only country which would have been thrown off its balance by the attraction of "public money" *à discrétion*. This false principle eats like a canker into the moral health and physical prosperity of the people. All classes "make a poor mouth," as it is expressively called in Ireland. They conceal their advantages, exaggerate their difficulties, and relax their exertions. The cottier does not sow his holding, the proprietor does not employ his poor in improving his estate, because by doing so they would disentitle themselves to their "share of the relief." The common wealth suffers both by the lavish consumption and the diminished production, and the bees of the hive, however they may redouble their exertions, must soon sink under its accumulated burden.... There is only one way in which the relief of the destitute ever has been, or ever will be, conducted consistently with the general welfare, and that is by *making it a local charge*. Those who know how to discriminate between the different claims for relief, then become actuated by a powerful motive to use that knowledge aright. They are spending

their own money. At the same time, those who have the means of employing the people in reproductive works have the strongest inducement given them to do so. The struggle now is to keep the poor off the rates, and if their labour only replaces the cost of their food, it is cheaper than having to maintain them in perfect idleness....

Our humble but sincere conviction is, that the appointed time of Ireland's regeneration is at last come. For several centuries we were in a state of open warfare with the native Irish, who were treated as foreign enemies, and were not admitted to the privileges and civilizing influences of English law, even when they most desired it.... Now, thank God, we are in a different position; and although many waves of disturbance must pass over us before that troubled sea can entirely subside, and time must be allowed for morbid habits to give place to a more healthy action, England and Ireland are, with one great exception, subject to equal laws; and so far as the maladies of Ireland are traceable to political causes, nearly every practical remedy has been applied. The deep and inveterate root of social evil remained, and this has been laid bare by a direct stroke of an all-wise and all-merciful Providence, as if this part of the case were beyond the unassisted power of man. Innumerable had been the specifics which the wit of man had devised; but even the idea of the sharp but effectual remedy by which the cure is likely to be effected had never occurred to any one. God grant that the generation to which this great opportunity has been offered may rightly perform its part, and that we may not relax our efforts until Ireland fully participates in the social health and physical prosperity of Great Britain, which will be the true consummation of their union!

Charles Trevelyan
The Irish Crisis
1848

The influential Times *newspaper strongly supported Trevelyan's line, as in this article on "the indolent preference of the Irish for relief over labour."*

Human agency is now denounced as instrumental in adding to the calamity inflicted by Heaven. It is no longer submission to Providence, but a murmur against the Government. The potatoes were blighted by a decree from on high, but labour is defrauded by the machinations of earthly power.... Such are the thanks that a Government gets for attempting to palliate great afflictions and satisfy corresponding demands by an inevitable but a ruinous beneficence....

The alarm of the populace in the provincial towns has arisen in some cases from the fact of the wages paid by Government being below the average standard of wages in the vicinity; in others, from the report that it is the intention to reduce them below that standard. This is the secret of he murmur. But how much does it disclose! How much does it indicate! It is the old thing; the old grievance is at the bottom; the old malady is breaking out. It is the national character, the national thoughtlessness, the national indolence. It is that which demands the attention of Governments, of patriots, and philanthropists, not a whit less than the potato disease. The Government provided work for a people who love it not. It made this the absolute condition of relief.... It knew that the [people] would at all times

T*he* Times *consigning Irish speeches to the waters of oblivion, 1849.*

rather be idle than toil.... It saw distinctly the prospect of more than half a nation becoming complacently dependent upon specious alms. There was but one way to avoid a calamity compared with which the potato blight is a trivial thing. This was to enjoin that work, slovenly and sluggishly performed—as the Government work was sure to be—should procure subsistence to the peasant, but nothing more. The Government was required to ward off starvation, not to pamper indolence; its duty was to encourage industry, not to stifle it; to stimulate others to give employment, not out-bid them, or drive them from the labour market....

But what would happen in other countries never does happen in Ireland. There the process as well as the motive of every action is inverted. Instead of increased exertion and renewed industry, passive submission and despondent indolence awaited a famine epoch....

Alas! the Irish peasant had tasted of famine and found that it was good. He saw the cloud looming in the distance and he hailed its approach. To him it teemed with goodly manna and salient waters. He wrapped himself up in the ragged mantle of inert expectancy and said that he trusted to Providence. But the deity of his faith was the Government—the manna of his hopes was a Parliamentary grant. He called his submission a religious obedience, and he believed it to be so. But it was the obedience of a religion which, by a small but material change, reversed the primaeval decree. It was a religion that holds, "Man shall *not* labour by the sweat of his brow."...

[T]here are ingredients in the Irish character which must be modified and corrected before either individuals or Governments can hope to raise the general condition of the people.... And this change cannot be effected until the landholders and squireens exert themselves. Had the smaller gentry resident in Ireland done their duty to their tenants and dependants...had they set the example of attention to their properties and improvement of their estates, the Irish would long ago have repudiated the potato. Neglected by others, they neglected themselves. Hence the universal prostration of self-complacent poverty and unrepining discontent.

We have a great faith in the virtues of good food.... The stomach is more than the mind a creature of habit. Accustom it to leeks or potatoes, it is indifferent to a generous diet. Once

habituate it to substantial solids, it rebels against leguminous impostures. The consequence is obvious.... He who is in danger of being starved by idleness will make one more struggle to earn his bread, his beef and his porter....

For our parts, we regard the potato blight as a blessing. When the Celts once cease to be potatophagi, they must become carnivorous. With the taste of meats will grow the appetite for them; with the appetite, the readiness to earn them. With this will come steadiness, regularity, and perseverance; unless, indeed, the growth of these qualities be impeded by the blindness of Irish patriotism, short-sighted indifference of petty landlords, or the random recklessness of Government benevolence....

Nothing will strike so deadly a blow, not only at the dignity of the Irish character, but also the elements of Irish prosperity, as a confederacy of rich proprietors to dun the national Treasury, and so to eke out from our resources that employment for the poor which they are themselves bound to provide, by every sense of duty, to a land from which they derive their incomes. It is too hard that the Irish landlord should come to ask charity of the English and Scottish mechanic, in a year in which the export of produce to England has been beyond all precedent extensive and productive. But it seems that those who forget all duties forget all shame.

The Times
22 September 1846

Irish landowners were infuriated by these attempts to put the blame for the Famine on their shoulders. Isaac Butt, a leading Irish Conservative, demanded more aid and greater landlord control over its spending. His disgust with British policies was to propel him towards support for Irish Home Rule.

[Peel's] arrangements recognized the duty of government to feed the people to the utmost extent to which all the resources of the empire could accomplish that end. That duty, under the more trying circumstances of this year, we are satisfied that Sir Robert Peel would have discharged, and by a larger expenditure of money, but still an expenditure utterly insignificant in comparison with the revenue of England, he would have fulfilled it with equal ease as he had done the year before....

The summer of 1846 saw the place of Sir Robert Peel filled by Lord John Russell.... We cannot believe that previous to the prorogation of parliament [Whig] ministers foresaw the full extent of the destitution which they had to meet. Ignorance of that extent is the only possible excuse for their measures. Their Labour Rate [Public Works] Act was, in truth, applying to meet the exigencies of a famine, the very principle of the Poor-Law of Queen Elizabeth, and applying it in the very worst possible way, compelling enormous waste of the resources of the country upon useless works; and we cannot help regarding as a great and a fatal mistake the determination to leave the supply of food entirely to the chances of private enterprise....

It is difficult to trace this history without indignation. We can under-

An idealized picture of rural relationships: a land agent visits a tenant cabin.

stand the verdict of the coroner's jury, who in days, when inquests were held in Ireland upon the bodies of men found dead upon the highway, returned upon the body of a man who died of starvation while toiling at the public works, and fell dead of exhaustion with the implements of labour in his hand, a verdict of murder against the ministers who had neglected the first responsibility of government. Can we wonder if the Irish people believe— *and believe it they do*—that the lives of those who have perished, and who will perish, have been sacrificed by a deliberate compact to the gains of English merchants, and if this belief has created among all classes a feeling of deep dissatisfaction, not only with the ministry but with English rule....

What can be more absurd, what can be more wicked, than for men professing attachment to an imperial Constitution to answer claims now put forward for state assistance to the unprecedented necessities of Ireland, by talking of Ireland being a drain upon the *English* treasury?... If the Union be not a mockery, there exists no such thing as an English treasury. The exchequer is the exchequer of the United Kingdom. ... How are these expectations to be realized...if, bearing our share of all imperial burdens—when calamity falls upon us we are to be told that we then recover our separate existence as a nation, just so far as to disentitle us to the state assistance which any portion of a nation visited with such a calamity had a right to expect from the governing power? If Cornwall had been visited with the scenes that have desolated Cork, would similar arguments been used? Would men have stood up and denied that Cornwall was entitled to have the whole country share the

extraordinary loss?...

All our measures are based upon the principle that this calamity ought to be regarded as an imperial one, and borne by the empire at large. If this be not conceded—if the state be not, as we have said, *our* government—if we are not to receive the assistance which government can render upon such an occasion—what alternative is there for any Irishman but to feel that the united parliament has abdicated the functions of government for Ireland, and to demand for his country that separate legislative existence, the necessity of which will then be fully proved.

Isaac Butt,
"The Famine in the Land,"
Dublin University Magazine, XXIX,
April 1847

The opinion of landowners was not uniform. Elizabeth Smith, the Scottish-born wife of a small landlord in County Wicklow, was damning of the Whigs but sympathetic to the idea of replacing the old aristocratic families with middle-class professionals. Her diary contrasts her own relief work with the indifference of other landowners.

21 January 1847: [T]he other resident landlords get on in the old way, the lowest wages, little work, no help in advice or otherwise; they may throw about a few pence when they are importuned by beggars, but they will take no trouble—they will do no *justice*. And there are large tracts of land belonging to absentees filled with squatters—all paupers—among whom a shilling is never spent, and who with the neglected peasantry of the indolent Landlords are all thrown upon us, the willing horses.... We have no right to look to richer England for help, no right

to expect government to take charge of our private affairs. We have brought our miseries upon ourselves; a long series of improvident management results in ruin. We who suffer may not in ourselves all of us, deserve this severe affliction, but we must bear the consequences of the evils permitted by our ancestors. The young race, rising, are aware of this moral retribution laid upon our generation; they bow to it, are prepared to meet it, to retrieve it, and no doubt the country will be raised a century the sooner from the frightful apathy into which all classes seemed to be sunk. But deeply must the nation suffer, and all that individuals can do is to work in their little circle to mitigate the misery....

30 October 1848: This season too very little cultivation is going forward; the peasantry are either in the poorhouse or gone to America; the farmers ditto; the proprietors ruined.... The poor law is partly in fault but by no means entirely; the potatoe failure is the determining cause, but the character of the people is at the bottom of the distress. What can then we say of English rule which has been over us for so many centuries and still leaves us so very far behind in the race of civilization.... We must have a new description of upper ranks who will be better models for those below them. The destitution by poverty and famine of the present generation is therefore a good feature of our deplorable case; the numbers will be thinned and the orders replaced in the gross by better men....

19 November 1848: It is the intention of the Government to root out the present proprietors of the soil en masse. They wish to finish them; perhaps they are not wrong; for as a class they have failed altogether to do their duty, but why crush the few righteous with the many erring. The English capitalists are waiting till the glut in the market still further reduces the value of the land.... This will annihilate our present aristocracy. Those of us who can struggle through will in time rise from the ashes fresh and vigorous, but how few will there be and how much must we first suffer....

The Irish Journals of Elizabeth Smith, 1840–1850, edited by David Thomson and Moyra McGusty, 1980

In 1847 the Catholic prelates issued a memorial to the Lord Lieutenant calling for greater relief aid and reform of the land system. The memorial's tone marked a compromise between the moderate conciliation of Archbishop Murray of Dublin and the outspoken nationalism of Archbishop MacHale of Tuam.

Sheweth—That memorialists, with sentiments of the most profound respect, approach your Excellency, filled with grief and alarm at the famine, which, for want of a sufficiency of food, has already set in in some of the western, southern, and in several other districts of Ireland, threatening a recurrence of all the horrors of the last season through which the people have passed, and that they are not without anxious solicitude for the distress which for want of sufficient employment is almost universally felt throughout the entire country....

Though memorialists are unwilling to detain your Excellency long by historical references, yet they feel it would be useful, with a view of providing vigorous and effectual remedies, to refer to the causes from which the distress has chiefly sprung. These causes are found in the unjust and penal enactments which, in other days, deprived the great bulk of the people of the rights of property, thus discouraging industry by debarring them from the enjoyment of its fruits; and though under the reign of her Gracious Majesty and that of her immediate predecessors, some of those laws have been repealed, their effects still remain, and are felt in the demoralisation and social derangement of which they were productive.

It is the violation of the principles of justice and of Christian morality from which those enactments had sprung and not to any innate indolence of the people that we may trace their depressed social condition, which, sinking gradually into still greater misery, terminated last year, by the failure of the potato crop, in the famine so tremendous in its havoc, and of which the present season threatens the appalling recurrence.

If the labourer is worthy of his hire, an axiom of natural as well as of revealed religion, and if doing to others as we should be done by be the golden standard of Christian morality, it would be a violation of those sacred axioms to appropriate the entire crops of the husbandman without compensating him for the seed or the labour expended on the cultivation of the soil.

Yet laws sanctioning such unnatural injustice, and, therefore, injurious to society, not only exist, but are extensively enforced with reckless and unrelenting rigour, while the sacred and indefeasible rights of life are forgotten amidst the incessant reclamations of the subordinate rights of property....

Hallowed as are the right of property, those of life are still more sacred, and rank as such in every well-regulated scale that adjusts the relative possessions of man; and if this scale had not been frequently reversed, we should have not so often witnessed in those heart-rending scenes of the evictions of the tenantry, "the oppressions that are done under the sun, the tears of the innocent having no comforter, and unable to resist violence, being destitute of help from any," which made the wise man "praise the dead rather than the living"....

In such an awful crisis, which threatens such destruction of human life, memorialists, anxious to preserve the souls of their flocks from crime, and society from the danger of disorganisation, beg respectfully, by imploring your Excellency to use your influence with her Majesty's govern-ment, to procure measures of relief commensurate with the magnitude of the calamity.

[A]n equitable arrangement of the relations between landlords and tenants, founded on commutative justice, appears to them so necessary that, without it they despair of ever seeing the poor sufficiently employed and protected, the land sufficiently cultivated, or the peace and prosperity of the country placed on a secure foundation. Large tracts of land capable of cultivation are now lying waste; the coasts abound in fish, which would give a large supply of food; encouragement to work those and other mines of wealth with which the country is teeming, would be well worthy of the solicitude of her Majesty's government. The poor are patient and long-enduring, though suffering grievously; they are looking with hope and confidence to her Majesty's government for relief, and a prompt and humane attention to their wants will save the lives and secure the lasting gratitude of her Majesty's most faithful people.

Memorial to his Excellency the Earl of Clarendon, *Freeman's Journal* 26 October 1847

The agrarian radical James Fintan Lalor took an apocalyptic view of the Famine, believing it had dissolved Irish society. He called for a social revolution against the landlords, and looked to Young Ireland to lead the struggle.

The failure of the potato, and consequent famine, is one of those events which come now and then to do the work of ages in a day, and change the very nature of an entire nation at once.... It has unsettled society to the foundation, deranged every interest, every class, every household. Every man's place and relation is altered; labour has left its track, and life lost its form. One entire class, the most numerous and important in Ireland, has already begun to give way....

The tenant-farmer of ten acres or under is being converted into an "independent labourer." But it is accomplishing something more than mere social derangement, or a dislocation of classes. It has come as if commissioned to produce, at length and not too soon, a dissolution of that state and order of existence in which we have heretofore been living. The constitution of society that has prevailed in this island can no longer maintain itself, or be maintained. It has been tried for generations; it has now, at least, been fully and finally tested; and the test has proved fatal. It was ever unsound and infirm; and is now breaking to pieces under the first severe experiment.... Nor heaven nor human nature will suffer it to be re-established or continue. If the earth,

Irish armed laborers waiting for the approach of a meal cart, 1847.

indeed, with all things therein was made wholly for the few and none of it for the many, then it may continue; if they be bound to submit in patience to perish of famine and famine-fever, then it may continue. But if all have a right to live, and to live in their own land among their own people; if they have a right to live in freedom and comfort on their own labour; if the humblest among them has a right to a full, secure and honest subsistence, not the knavish and beggarly subsistence of the poor-house, then that constitution cannot and it shall not be re-established again. When society fails to perform its duty and fulfil its office of providing for its people; it must take another and more effective form, or it must cease to exist. When its members begin to die out under destitution—when they begin to perish in thousands under famine and the effects of famine—when they begin to desert and fly from the land in hundreds of thousands under the force and fear of deadly famine—then it is time to see it is God's will that society should stand dissolved, and assume another shape and action; and he works his will by human hands and natural agencies. This case has arisen even now in Ireland…. The potato was our sole and only capital, to live and work on, to make much or little of; and on it the entire social economy of this country was founded, formed and supported. That system and state of things can never again be resumed or restored; not even should the potato return. A new…social order [is] to be arranged; a new people to be organised. Or otherwise that people itself is about to become extinct. Either of these is inevitable; and either is desirable. In condition and character and conduct, a stain to earth, a scandal among the nations, a shame to nature, a grievance

to Heaven, this people has been for ages past—a dark spot in the path of the sun. Nature and Heaven can bear it no longer. To any one who either looks to an immediate directing Providence, or trusts to a settled course of natural causes, it is clear that this island is about to take existence under a new tenure; or else that Nature has issued her decree —often issued heretofore against nations and races, and ever for the same crime— that one other imbecile and cowardly people shall cease to exist, and no longer cumber the earth.

James Fintan Lalor
"A New Nation," *The Nation*
24 April 1847

Not to repeal the Union, then, but to repeal the Conquest—not to disturb or dismantle the empire, but to abolish it forever—not to fall back on '82 but act up to '48—not to resume or restore an old constitution, but to found a new nation, and raise up a free people, and strong as well as free, and secure as well as strong, based on a peasantry rooted like rocks in the soil of the land—this is my object.…

The principle I state, and mean to stand upon, is this, that the entire ownership of Ireland, moral and material, up to the sun, and down to the centre, is vested of right in the people of Ireland; that they, and none but they, are the land-owners and law-makers of this island; that all laws are null and void not made by them; and all titles to land invalid not conferred and confirmed by them; and that this full right of ownership may and ought to be asserted and enforced by any and all means which God has put in the power of man.

James Fintan Lalor
The Irish Felon, 24 June 1848

Contemporary Literature

Many Irish turned to poetry, prose, and song as a way of venting grief and anger during the Famine years.

Songs in the Irish language, which is still spoken today in parts of the country, provide the most authentic record of the feelings of the poor. "Amhrán na bPrátaí Dubha" ("The Song of the Black Potatoes") by Máire Ní Dhroma of Ring, County Waterford, in original and translation by Cormac Ó Gráda here, expresses both the depths of piety and the anger at social injustice, that were aroused by the Famine.

Siad na prátaí dubha do dhein ár
    gcomharsana a scaipeadh uainn,
Do chuir sa phoorhouse iad, is anonn
    thar na farraigí;
I Reilig a' tSléibhe tá na céadta acu
    treascartha,
Is uaisle na bhflaitheas go ngabha a
    bpáirt.
A Dhia na glóire fóir agus freagair sinn
Scaoil ár nglasa agus réitíg ar gcás,
Ar an mbeatha arís, ó do chroí go
    gcasfar í,
San poorhouse go leagair anuas ar lár.

Más mar gheall ar ár bpeacaí claonmhar
    tháinig an chéim seo eadrainn,
Osgail ár gcroíthe 'gus díbir an
    ghanghaid as!
Leig braon beag ded' naoimhsprid arís
    chum ár gcneasaithe,
Is uaisle na bhflaitheas go ré ar gcás.
Níl aon chuimhne againne oíche ná
    maidin ort,
Ach ar ainnis a' tsaoil ag déanamh
    marbhna
A Íosa Críost, go dtógair dínn an
    scamall seo
Go mbéimis dod amharcadh gach am
    den lá.

Tá na bochta seo Éireann ag plé leis
    an ainnise
Buairt is anacair is pianta báis,
Leanaí bochta ag béiceadh is ag

Women on a soup line, 1847.

screadadh gach maidin
Ocras fada orthu is gan dada le fáil.
Is ní hé Dia cheap riamh an obair seo,
Daoine bochta do chur le fuacht is
  le fán,
Iad a chur sa phoorhouse go dúbhach
  is glas orthu,
Lánúineacha pósta is iad scartha go bás.

Na leanaí óga thógfaidís suas le macanais
Sciobtaí uathu iad gan trua gan taise
  dhóibh.
At bheagán lóin ach soup na hainnise
Gan mháthair le freagairt dóibh dá
  bhfaighdís bás.
A Rí na Trua 's a Uain ghil bheannaithe,
Féach an ainnise atá 'nár gcrá.
Is ná leig ar strae uait féin an t-anam
  bocht,
'Sa fheabhas a cheannaigh tú féin sa
  pháis.

Mo thrua móruaisle a bhfuil mórán
  coda acu
Gan tabhairt sásaimh san obair seo le
  Rí na nGrás;
Ach ag feall ar bhochta Dé nach bhfuair
  riamh aon saibhreas
Ach ag síorobair dóibh ó aois go bás.
Bíonn siad ar siúl ar maidin, ar an dóigh
  sin dóibh,
Is as sin go tráthnóna ag cur cuiríní
  allais díobh
Nil aon mhaith ina dícheall muna mbíd
  cuíosach, seasmhach
Ach téigí abhaile is beidh bhur dtithe
  ar lár.

'Twas the black potatoes that scattered
  our people
Facing the poorhouse or overseas
  emigration.
And in the mountain cemetery do they
  in hundreds lie,
And God in heaven relieve our situation.
O! King of Glory, hear and answer us,

From bondage save us, and come to
  our aid,
And send us bread, as we cry in misery,
And may the poorhouse be in ashes laid.

If for our sins we pay this penalty,
Open our hearts, that they may be
  cleansed!
One drop of Thy Blood send to
  comfort us,
In grief and hunger we are sore dismayed.
It is not on You we are meditating,
But on the wickedness of this life,
Oh King of Pity remove this cloud
  from us,
So that we are imagining you each hour
  of day!

The poor of Ireland are in great misery
Worry, and woe, and pains of death
Children screaming and wailing
Long without food and none to be got.
This business was no part of God's plan,
Scattering the poor in grief and pain,
The poorhouse gates clanging closed
  on them,
And married couples separated for life.

The children they reared, with parent's
  care for them,
The poorhouse bare doth rudely tear
  from them.
Or should they die no cry their mother
  hears,
Though they be lying near, by hunger
  slain!
O God of Pity and the blessed Lamb
  of love,
Look down from Heaven above on
  our ills,
Oh Shepherd, keep us now from straying
Whom Thy bitter pain brought on
  Judea's hills.

Oh pity the proud ones, all earth
  possessing

That for these distresses must surely pay,
Oh, sad their fate, who the poor
  oppressing
Do richer grow by their moans each day.
They work for them from the break
  of day
From then till evening sweating bands
  of sweat
Their labor has to be hard and steady,
Even so they go home to see their houses
  knocked down.

*English-language ballads also expressed
popular sentiments. This emigration
song dates from about 1847.*

Good people on you I call, give ear
  to these lines you soon shall hear;
I'm caused to weep deprived of sleep
  for parting from my relations dear;
My hardships here I can't endure,
  there's nothing here but slavery,

A priest blessing departing emigrants, 1851.

I will take my lot and leave this spot
  and try the land of liberty.

Farewell dear Erin, fare thee well, that
  once was call'd the Isle of Saints,
For here no longer can I dwell, I'm
  going to cross the stormy sea,
For to live here I can't endure, there's
  nothing here but slavery,
My heart's oppress'd, I can find no rest,
  I will try the land of liberty.

My father holds five acres of land, it
  was not enough to support us all,
Which banishes me from my native land,
  to old Ireland dear I bid farewell.
My hardships here I can't endure,
  since here I no longer can stay
I take my lot and leave this spot and
  try the land of liberty.

My love, you know that trade is low,
  provision's they're exceedingly high,
We see the poor from door to door
  craving their wants we can't supply,

We hear their moans, their sighs and
    groans, with children naked, cold
    and bare,
Craving relief, it renews my grief as
    we have nothing for to spare.

So now my dear you need not fear
    the dangers of the raging sea,
If your mind is bent I am content, so
    now prepare and come away.
My dear, if you'll agree to marry me,
    I'll quickly prepare,
We'll join our hands in wedlock's bands
    and we will stay no longer here.
It was in the year of '46 I was forced
    to leave my native land,
To old Ireland I bid adieu and to
    my fond relations all,
But now I'm in America, no rents
    or taxes we pay at all,
So now I bid a long farewell to my
    native and old Donegal.

             Anonymous
"The Emigrant's Farewell to Donegal"
             c. 1847

*Sir Samuel Ferguson, an Irish Protestant
lawyer and antiquarian, drew on the
satirical tradition of Dean Swift and
Samuel Johnson in writing his verse attack
on "political economy." It is structured
around an imaginary conversation between
the ruthless English ECONOMIST and
the Irish landlord INHERITOR, on how
to deal with PAUPER.*

"Take with you," said ECONOMIST,
    "that we
Are living in the nineteenth century,
Not in the days of saints or anchorites;
Days, did I say?—say rather in the nights!
When mendicancy in the state demands
A scientific treatment at our hands.
This vagrant now the countryside
    imbues
With idle habits and the love of news;

Pernicious tales from house to house
    imports
Of births, deaths, marriages, and
    country sports—
Seditious rumours, threats and bulletins
O' the Ribbon-lodge, and smith's-forge
    magazines;
Idles the schoolboys with his tricks,
The adult workers with his politics;
And so, at public charge, with little
    pains
Himself, his vermin and his dog
    maintains.
Now, trust your Irish Poor-Reform
    to me,
And speedily (his terrier hanged)
    you'll see
How science shall economize your
    rogue,
And save society the keep of's dog;
Shall utilise him, sir, in such a sort,
That this one beggar haply shall support
Stead of the vermin who now suck
    his blood,
Of paid official bloodsuckers a brood
More numerous far, whose legions
    swarming thick
O'er all parts of the body politic,
Shall in a systematic way apply
Anti-phlogistics and phlebotomy;
Or, if the patient sigh for nobler wants,
A rousing course of counter irritants,
Till all the members of your
    Commonwealth
Are bled and blistered into perfect
    health.
No longer, then, your country's cure
    defer—
Make haste, appoint one Chief
    Commissioner
To supervise all Beggarland's concerns,
Fifty inspectors, chiefs, and subalterns;
Fifty collectors, with good sureties,
To gather in the dues: than add to these
Five hundred guardians, vice and
    volunteer—

Five hundred clerks at fifty pounds
    a-year;
Five hundred masters, and five hundred
    dames,
Five hundred Health-Board doctors
    of all names;
Five hundred builders from the Board
    of Works,
Five hundred chaplains, and five
    hundred clerks."
"Sir," said INHERITOR, "I'd not
    be rash,
But sure this cure would cost a deal
    of cash"?

"Not half so much," ECONOMIST
    replies,
"As now is spent on PAUPER'S
    luxuries.…"

Deem not, O generous English hearts,
    who gave
Your noble aid our sinking isle to save,
This breast, though heated in its
    country's feud,
Owns aught towards you but perfect
    gratitude.
For every dish retrenched from homely
    boards,
For every guinea from prudent hoards,
For every feast deferred, and jewel sold,
May God increase your stores a
    hundred-fold.…
But, frankly while we thank you all
    who sent
Your alms, so thank we not your
    Parliament,
Who, what they gave, from treasures
    of our own
Gave, if you call it giving, this half-loan,
Half-gift from the recipients to
    themselves
Of their own millions, be they tens
    or twelves;
Our own as well as yours; our Irish
    brows

Had sweated for them; though your
    Commons House,
Forgetting your four hundred millions
    debt,
When first in partnership our nations
    met,
Against our twenty-four (you then
    twofold
The poorer people)—call them British
    gold.
No; for these drafts on our united banks
We owe no gratitude, and give no thanks,
More than you'd give to us, if Dorsetshire
Or York a like assistance should require;
Or than you gave us, when, to
    compensate
Your slave-owners, you charged our
    common state
Twice the amount; no, but we rather
    give
Our curses, and will give them while
    we live,
To that pernicious blind conceit, and
    pride,
Wherewith the aids we asked, you
    misapplied.…

             Sir Samuel Ferguson
"Inheritor and Economist: a Poem," 1849

Of all the poets writing at the time, James Clarence Mangan came closest to articulating the horrors of the Famine with a new voice. "Siberia" expressed both his dread of his own impending death, and the desolation and despair of the landscape around him.

In Siberia's wastes
    The Ice-wind's breath
Woundeth like the toothed steel;
    Lost Siberia doth reveal
Only blight and death.

Blight and death alone.
    No summer shines.
Night is interblent with Day.

A famine funeral in County Cork, 1847.

In Siberia's wastes alway
  The blood blackens, the heart pines.

In Siberia's wastes
  No tears are shed,
For they freeze within the brain.
Nought is felt but dullest pain,
  Pain acute, yet dead;

Pain as in a dream,
  When years go by
Funeral-paced, yet fugitive,
When man lives, and doth not live,
  Doth not live—nor die.

In Siberia's wastes
  Are sands and rocks.
Nothing blooms of green or soft,
  But the snow-peaks rise aloft
And gaunt ice-blocks.

And the exile there
  Is one with those;
They are part, and he is part,
For the sands are in his heart,
  And the killing snows.
Therefore in those wastes

None curse the Czar.
Each man's tongue is cloven by
The North Blast, that heweth nigh
  With sharp scymitar.

And such doom each drees,
  Till, hunger-gnawn,
And cold-slain, he at length sinks there,
Yet scarce more a corpse than ere
  His last breath was drawn.
                    James Clarence Mangan
                        "Siberia," 1846

Lady Wilde (Jane Francesca Elgee, mother of the famous wit Oscar Wilde) shared the prophetic and millenarian vision of the romantic nationalist poets who published regularly in The Nation.

Weary men, what reap ye?—Golden
  corn for the stranger.
What sow ye?—Human corses that
  wait for the avenger.
Fainting forms, hunger-stricken, what
  see you in the offing?
Stately ships to bear our food away,
  amid the stranger's scoffing.
There's a proud array of soldiers—
  what do they round your door?
They guard our masters' granaries from

the thin hands of the poor.
Pale mothers, wherefore weeping—
  Would to God that we were dead;
Our children swoon before us, and
  we cannot give them bread.

Little children, tears are strange upon
  your infant faces,
God meant you but to smile within
  your mother's soft embraces.
Oh! we know not what is smiling, and
  we know not what is dying;
We're hungry, very hungry, and we
  cannot stop our crying.
And some of us grow cold and white—
  we know not what it means;
But, as they lie beside us, we tremble
  in our dreams.
There's a gaunt crowd on the highway
  —are ye come to pray to man,
With hollow eyes that cannot weep, and
  for words your faces wan?

No; the blood is dead within our veins
  —we care not now for life;
Let us die hid in the ditches, far from
  children and from wife;
We cannot stay and listen to their
  raving, famished cries—
Bread! Bread! Bread! and none to still
  their agonies.
We left our infants playing with their
  dead mother's hand:
We left our maidens maddened by the
  fever's scorching brand:
Better, maiden, thou were strangled in
  thy own dark-twisted tresses—
Better, infant, thou wert smothered
  in thy mother's first caresses.

We were fainting in our misery, but
  God will hear our groan:
Yet, if fellow-man desert us, will He
  hearken from His Throne?
Accursed are we in our own land,
  yet toil we still and toil;

But the stranger reaps our harvest—
  the alien owns our soil.
O Christ! how have we sinned, that
  on our native plains
We perish houseless, naked, starved,
  with branded brow, like Cain's?
Dying, dying wearily, with torture
  sure and slow—
Dying, as a dog would die, by the
  wayside as we go.

One by one they're falling round us,
  their pale faces to the sky;
We've no strength left to dig them
  graves—there let them lie.
The wild bird, if he's stricken, is
  mourned by the others,
But we—we die in Christian land—
  we die amid our brothers,
In the land which God has given, like
  a wild beast in his cave,
Without a tear, a prayer, a shroud, a
  coffin or a grave.
Ha! but think ye the contortions on
  each livid face ye see,
Will not be read on judgement-day
  by eyes of Deity?

We are wretches, famished, scorned,
  human tools to build your pride,
But God will yet take vengeance for
  the souls for whom Christ died.
Now is your hour of pleasure—bask
  ye in the world's caress;
But our whitening bones against ye
  will rise as witnesses,
From the cabins and the ditches, in
  their charred, uncoffin'd masses,
For the Angel of the Trumpet will
  know them as he passes.
A ghastly, spectral army, before the
  great God we'll stand,
And arraign ye as our murderers, the
  spoilers of our land.

           Lady Wilde ("Speranza")
           "The Famine Year," 1847

One of Ireland's best-known prose writers by the 1840s, William Carleton drew on his own memories of earlier Irish famines for The Black Prophet. *The book was intended to shock his readers into a more generous response in 1847. These passages describe the practices of a village "gombeen-man," or petty money-lender, and the ravages of fever.*

There is to be found in Ireland, and, we presume, in all other countries, a class of hardened wretches, who look forward to a period of dearth as to one of great gain and advantage, and who contrive, by exercising the most heartless and diabolical principles, to make the sickness, famine, and general desolation which scourge their fellow-creatures, so many sources of successful extortion and rapacity, and consequently of gain to themselves. They are country misers or moneylenders, who are remarkable for keeping meal until the arrival of what is termed a hard year, or a dear summer, when they sell it out at enormous or usurious prices....

About half a mile from the residence of the Sullivans, lived a remarkable man of this class, named Darby Skinadre. In appearance he was lank and sallow, with a long, thin, parched-looking face, and a miserable crop of yellow beard....

Skinadre, on the day we write of, was reaping a rich harvest from the miseries of the unhappy people. In a lower room of his house...he stood over his scales, weighing out with a dishonest and parsimonious hand, the scanty pittance which poverty enabled the wretched creatures to purchase from him.... There stood Skinadre, like the very Genius of Famine, surrounded by distress, raggedness, feeble hunger, and tottering disease, in all the various aspects of pitiable suffering, hopeless desolation, and that agony of the heart which impresses wildness upon the pale cheek, makes the eye at once dull and eager, parches the mouth, and gives to the voice of misery tones that are hoarse and hollow. There he stood, striving to blend consolation with deceit, and, in the name of religion and charity, subjecting the helpless wretches to fraud and extortion. Around him was misery, multiplied into all her most appalling shapes. Fathers of families were there, who could read in each other's faces, too truly, the gloom and anguish that darkened the brow and wrung the heart. The strong man, who had been not long before a comfortable farmer, now stood dejected and apparently broken-down, shorn of his strength without a trace of either hope or spirit; so wofully shrunk away too, from his superfluous apparel that the spectators actually wondered to think that this was the large man, of such powerful frame, whose feats of strength had so often heretofore filled them with amazement. But, alas! what will not sickness and hunger do?...

It is impossible, however, to describe the various aspects and claims of misery which presented themselves at Skinadre's house. The poor people flitted to and fro, silently and dejectedly, wasted, feeble, and sickly—sometimes in small groups of twos and threes, and sometimes a solitary individual might be seen hastening with earnest but languid speed, as if the life of some dear child or beloved parent, of a husband or wife, or, perhaps, the lives of a whole family, depended upon his or her arrival with food....

At this precise period, the state of the country was frightful beyond belief; for it is well known that the mortality of the season...was considerably greater than that which even cholera occasioned in its worst and most malignant ravages. Indeed the latter was not attended by such a tedious and lingering train of miseries as that which, in so many woful shapes, surrounded typhus fever. The appearance of cholera was sudden, and its operations quick, and although, on that account, it was looked upon with tenfold terror, yet for this very reason the consequences which it produced were by no means so full of affliction and distress, nor presented such strong and pitiable claims on human aid and sympathy as did those of typhus. In one case the victim was cut down by a sudden stroke, which occasioned a shock or moral paralysis both to himself and the survivors…that might be almost said to neutralize its own afflictions. In the other, the approach was comparatively so slow and gradual, that all the sympathies and afflictions were allowed full and painful time to reach the utmost limits of human suffering.…

In fact, Ireland, during the season, or rather the year we are describing, might be compared to one vast lazar [leper]-house filled with famine, disease and death. The very skies of heaven were hung with the black drapery of the grave, for never since, nor in the memory of man before it, did the clouds present shapes of such gloomy and funereal import. Hearses, coffins, long funeral processions, and all the dark emblems of mortality were reflected, as it were, on the sky, from the terrible works of pestilence and famine which were going forward on the earth beneath it.

William Carleton
The Black Prophet, 1847

The English novelist Anthony Trollope was employed as a post office official in Ireland during the Famine. He was a strong defender of government policy at the time, *but softened his opinions somewhat when he came to depict the events in fictional form some years later.*

At the gate, just as Herbert was about to remount his horse, they were encountered by a sight which for years past has not been uncommon in the south of Ireland, but which had become frightfully common during the last two or three months. A woman was standing there, of whom you could hardly say that she was clothed, though she was involved in a mass of rags which covered her nakedness. Her head was all uncovered, and her wild black hair was streaming round her face. Behind her back hung two children enveloped among the rags in some mysterious way; and round her on the road stood three others, of whom the two younger were almost absolutely naked. The eldest of the five was not above seven. They all had the same wild black eyes, and wild elfish straggling locks; but neither the mother nor the children were comely. She was short and broad in the shoulders, though wretchedly thin; her bare legs seemed to be of nearly the same thickness up to the knee, and the naked limbs of the children were like yellow sticks.…

When Herbert and Clara reached the gate they found this mother with her five children crouching at the ditch-side, although it was still mid-winter. They had seen him enter the demesne, and were now waiting with the patience of poverty for his return.

"An' the holy Virgin guide an' save you, my lady," said the woman, almost frightening Clara by the sudden way in which she came forward, "an' you too, Misther Herbert; and for the love of heaven do something for a poor crathur whose five starving childher have not had wholesome food within their lips for the last week past.".…

But Herbert had learned deep lessons of political economy, and was by no means disposed to give promiscuous charity on the road-side.… "But you know that we will not give money. They will take you in at the poorhouse at Kanturk."

"Is it the poorhouse, yer honor?"

"Or, if you get a ticket from your priest they will give you meal twice a week a Clady. You know that. Why do you not go to Father Connellan?"

"Is it the mail? An' shure an' haven't I had it, the last month past; nothin' else; nor a taste of a praty or a dhrop of milk for nigh a month, and now look at the childher. Look at them, my lady. They are dyin' by the very roadside." And she undid the bundle at her back, and laying the two babes down on the road showed that the elder of them was in truth in a fearful state. It was a child nearly two years of age, but its little legs seemed to have withered away; its cheeks were wan, and yellow and sunken, and the two teeth which it had already cut were seen with terrible plainness through its emaciated lips. Its head and forehead were covered with sores; and then the mother, moving aside the rags, showed that its back and legs were in the same state. "Look to that," she said, almost with scorn. "That's what the mail has done—my black curses be upon it, and the day that it first came nigh the counthry." And then she again covered the child and began to resume her load.

"Do give her something, Herbert, pray do," said Clara, with her whole face suffused with tears.…

Herbert Fitzgerald, from the first moment of his interrogating the woman, had of course known that he would give her somewhat. In spite of all his political economy, there were but few days in which he did not empty his pocket of his loose silver, with these culpable deviations from his theoretical philosophy. But yet he felt that it was his duty to insist on his rules, as far as his heart would allow him to do so. It was a settled thing at their relief committee that there should be no giving away of money to chance applicants for alms. What money each had to bestow would go twice further by being brought to the general fund—by being expended with forethought and discrimination. This was the system which all attempted, which all resolved to adopt who were then living in the south of Ireland. But the system was impracticable, for it required frames of iron and hearts of adamant. It was impossible not to waste money in almsgiving.

"Oh, Herbert!" said Clara, imploringly, as the woman prepared to start.

"Bridget, come here," said Herbert.… "Your child is very ill, and therefore I will give you something to help you," and he gave her a shilling and two sixpences.… "Go on now, my good woman," said he, "and take your children where they may be warm. If you will be advised by me, you will go to the Union at Kanturk." And so the woman passed on still blessing them. Very shortly after this none of them required pressing to go to the workhouse. Every building that could be arranged for the purpose was filled to overflowing as soon as it was ready. But the worst of the famine had not come upon them as yet. And then Herbert rode back to Castle Richmond.

Anthony Trollope
Castle Richmond
1860

Modern Literature

The terrible story of the Famine lives on in the memory— and work—of 20th-century Irish writers.

Liam O'Flaherty's 1937 novel Famine, *though historically flawed, remains the most vivid and moving prose account of the catastrophe. In this extract the heroine prepares to flee to America.*

Mary looked along the ditch. It was becoming quite light now. The clamour of turning wheels and of hooves was quite near. Pools of light were spread over the sea.

"It's dawn," Mary said, looking at the housekeeper in a frightened way. "I thought there would be...."

Then she bit her lip and wrinkled her forehead, afraid that she had said too much. She laughed.

"Huh!," said the housekeeper angrily. "It's kind sister for you to have little nature in you, laughing in a place like this."

"Ah, no," Mary said, "it's not for a mean reason I am laughing, but I am light in the head. I thought I'd never get here alive. There is no one alive up in Black Valley except Brian and Maggie. The place is empty. I left them something in the bag. That's all. I saw no one in the village, but I heard a great screeching from fighting dogs. It's like a dead place. Father Geelan said that Johnny Hynes [the gombeen man] is gone."

"The curse of Cromwell on him," said the housekeeper.... "Money can't buy everything. They have made enough of it on account of this famine. That ship that's taking people to America today brought him another load of corn from Philadelphia."

"Is there a ship going today?" Mary cried, gripping the housekeeper by the arm.

"There is," said the housekeeper mournfully. "There is one going every few days now. It's over there in America

I should be now, only for the sickness that laid me low. The money was gone on lodgings before I got better…. Everyone is gone that had the passage money. It's the richest that are gone and only the scum left. They will all die."

Mary was now trembling with excitement and she was looking anxiously from side to side.

"I saw dead people on the road," she said, as if thinking aloud. "One person I met said that Colonel Bodkin, the magistrate, is giving out food, but it's only for his tenants. The same person said that Father Roche is as thin as a shadow. He gives his dinner to the beggars every day. Colonel Bodkin has a watchman at his gate. The person said that the government would start the works again, but there would be no one strong enough to work at the tasks."

The noise of cart-wheels and of hooves had now become mingled with the sharp sound of cracking whips and the shouts of men. The people lying in the ditch were roused by the tumult. Some of them sat up and groaned. Others tossed about on the ground. A few did not move at all. A little girl was shaking her mother, to whom she called piteously.

"Lord save us!" said the woman from Garrymore. "It's like the dead rising from their graves with the break of day. Oh! Look at the red coats on horseback."

Three horsemen came riding from the east, along the edge of the tall shore grass. The hooves of their horses threw up little blobs of sand…. A convoy of carts followed the horsemen. Soldiers marched on either side of the carts. The men on horseback had swords and the footmen had carbines. Two of the soldiers on horseback were singing. The carts were loaded with sacks.

Suddenly a tall man rose from the far end of the ditch near the shore road. He was half naked. He raised his right hand with the fist clenched. A piece of his sleeve hung down by his naked elbow.

"Robbers!" he cried, as he shook his upraised fist at the convoy. "Ye are taking the people's harvest out of the country. Ye are stealing our corn and we dying of hunger. We are laid low now but we will rise again. We'll crush the tyrants that suck our blood. The people will rise again."

Then an angry murmur, like a cheer of defiance, passed along the ditch. Other figures rose up and threatened the convoy with their clenched fists. Excited by this murmur the half naked man ran forward shouting. One of the soldiers struck him on the head with a carbine. The man fell. The convoy passed on quickly. Now there were many soldiers singing in unison. A woman ran out from the ditch and began to drag the fallen man.

Liam O'Flaherty
Famine
1937

For many modern Irish poets, the Famine remains a part of the physical and mental landscape of Ireland.

Crossing the shallow holdings high
  above sea
Where few birds nest, the luckless foot
  may pass
From the bright safety of experience
Into the terror of the hungry grass.

Here in a year when poison from the air
First withered in despair the growth
  of spring

Some skull-faced wretch whom nettle
  could not save
Crept on four bones to his last
  scattering,

Crept, and the shrivelled heart which
  drove his thought
Towards platters brought in hospitality
Burst as the wizened eyes measured
  the miles
Like dizzy walls forbidding him
  the city.

Little the earth reclaimed from that
  poor body,
And yet remembering him the place
  has grown
Bewitched and the thin grass he
  nourishes
Racks with his famine, sucks marrow
  from the bone.

Donagh MacDonagh
"The Hungry Grass"
1947
from The Penguin Book of Irish Verse
Edited by Brendan Kennelly
1970

I.
A mechanical digger wrecks the drill,
Spins up a dark shower of roots and
  mould.
Labourers swarm in behind, stoop
  to fill
Wicker creels. Fingers go dead in
  the cold.
Like crows attacking crow-black fields,
  they stretch
A higgledy line from hedge to headland;
Some pairs keep breaking ragged ranks
  to fetch
A full creel to the pit and straighten,
  stand

Tall for a moment but soon stumble
  back

To fish a new load from the crumbled
  surf.
Heads bow, trunks bend, hands fumble
  towards the black
Mother. Processional stooping through
  the turf

Recurs mindlessly as autumn.
  Centuries
Of fear and homage to the famine god
Toughen the muscles behind their
  humbled knees,
Make a seasonal altar of the sod.

II.
Flint-white, purple. They lie scattered
like inflated pebbles. Native
to the black hutch of clay
where the halved seed shot and clotted
these knobbed and slit-eyed tubers seem
the petrified hearts of drills. Split
by the spade, they show white as cream.

Good smells exude from crumbled
  earth.
The rough bark of humus erupts
knots of potatoes (a clean birth)
whose solid feel, whose wet inside
promises taste of ground and root.
To be piled in pits; live skulls,
  blind-eyed.

III.
Live skulls, blind-eyed, balanced on
wild higgledy skeletons
scoured the land in 'forty-five,
wolfed the blighted root and died.
The new potato, sound as stone,
putrefied when it had lain
three days in the long clay pit.
Millions rotted along with it.

Mouths tightened in, eyes died hard,
faces chilled to a plucked bird.
In a million wicker huts
beaks of famine snipped at guts.

Women digging a potato field, mid-19th century.

A people hungering from birth,
grubbing, like plants, in the bitch
    earth,
were grafted with a great sorrow.
Hope rotted like a marrow.

Stinking potatoes fouled the land,
pits turned pus into filthy mounds:
and where potato diggers are
you still smell the running sore.

IV.
Under a gay flotilla of gulls
The rhythm deadens, the workers
    stop.
Brown bread and tea in bright
    canfuls
Are served for lunch. Dead-beat,
    they flop

Down in the ditch and take their fill,
Thankfully breaking timeless fasts;
Then, stretched on the faithless
    ground, spill
Libations of cold tea, scatter crusts.

Seamus Heaney
"At a Potato Digging"
from *Death of a Naturalist*
1966

There's not a chance now that I might
    recover
one syllable of what that sick man said,
tapping upon my great-grandmother's
    shutter,
and begging, I was told, a piece
    of bread;
for on his tainted breath there hung
    infection

rank from the cabins of the stricken
    west,
the spores from black potato-stalks,
    the spittle
mottled with poison in his rattling chest;
but she who, by her nature, quickly
    answered,
accepting in return the famine-fever;
and that chance meeting, that brief
    confrontation,
conscribed me of the Irishry for ever.

Though much I cherish lies outside
    their vision,
and much they prize I have no claim
    to share,
yet in that woman's death I found
    my nation;
the old wound aches and shews its
    fellow scar.

John Hewitt
"The Scar"
from *The Collected Poems of John Hewitt*
Edited by Frank Ormsby, 1991

That the science of cartography
    is limited
—and not simply by the fact that
    this shading of
forest cannot show the fragrance
    of balsam,
the gloom of cypresses
is what I wish to prove.

When you and I were first in love
    we drove
to the borders of Connacht
and entered a wood there.

Look down you said: this was once
    a famine road.
I looked down at ivy and the scutch
    grass
rough-cast stone had
disappeared into as you told me
in the second winter of their ordeal, in

1847, when the crop had failed twice,
Relief Committees gave
the starving Irish such roads to build.

Where they died, there the road
    ended

and ends still and when I take down
the map of this island, it is never so
I can say here is
the masterful, the apt rendering of

A street in Youghal, County Wexford, 1870s.

the spherical as flat, nor
an ingenious design which persuades
    a curve
into a plane,

but to tell myself again that
the line which says woodland and
    cries hunger

and gives out among sweet pine and
    cypress,
and finds no horizon

will not be there.

Eavan Boland
"That the Science of
Cartography is Limited," 1994

The Historical Debate

The meaning of the Great Famine has been contested by politicians and historians from the 1850s to the present day.

The Famine has been to different writers a source of nationalist anger, a historical problem to be coolly dissected and demythologized, and a reminder of the realities of hunger and poverty in the modern world.

John Mitchel strongly condemned British policy in Ireland.

[A] million and a half of men, women and children, were carefully, prudently, and peacefully *slain* by the English government. They died of hunger in the midst of abundance, which their own hands created; and it is quite immaterial to distinguish those who perish in the agonies of famine itself from those who died of typhus fever, which in Ireland is always caused by famine.

Further, I have called it an artificial famine: that is to say, it was a famine which desolated a rich and fertile island, that produced every year abundance and superabundance to sustain all her people and many more. The English, indeed, call that famine a "dispensation of Providence;" and ascribe it entirely to the blight of the potatoes. But potatoes failed in like manner all over Europe; yet there was no famine save in Ireland. The British account of the matter, then, is first, a fraud—second, a blasphemy. The Almighty, indeed, sent the potato blight, but the English created the famine....

The subjection of Ireland is now probably assured until some external shock shall break up that monstrous commercial firm, the British Empire; which, indeed, is a bankrupt firm, and trading on false credit, and embezzling the goods of others, or robbing on the highway, from Pole to Pole, but its doors are not yet shut; its cup of abomination is not yet running over. If any American has read this narrative,

The "Famine Queen"—an attack on Queen Victoria published in Paris in 1900.

however, he will never wonder hereafter when he hears an Irishman in America fervently curse the British Empire. So long as this hatred and horror shall last—so long as our island refuses to become, like Scotland, a contented province of her enemy, Ireland is not finally subdued. The passionate aspiration for Irish nationhood will outlive the British empire.

John Mitchel
The Last Conquest of Ireland (Perhaps)
1860

The Revisionist response: from the foreword to The Great Famine.

It is difficult to know how many men and women died in Ireland in the famine years between 1845 and 1852. Perhaps all that matters is the certainty that many, very many, died. The Great Famine was not the first nor the last period of acute distress in Irish history. The Great Famine may be seen as but a period of greater misery in a prolonged age of suffering, but it has left an enduring mark on the folk memory because of its duration and severity. The famine is seen as the source of many woes, the symbol of the exploitation of a whole nation by its oppressors. If only because of its importance in the shaping of Irish national thought, the famine deserves examination. But it was much more than a mere symbol....

In the year 1848, Charles Gavan Duffy, the Young Irelander, full of anger and mortification could cry out that the famine was nothing less than, "a fearful murder committed on the mass of the people." That indictment has come down to us alive and compelling in the writings of John Mitchel. This famine, which saw the destruction of the cottier

class and forced some 3,000,000 people to live on charity in the year 1847, was something that went to the very basis of Irish society. It is easy to say, at a distance of a century, that men like Mitchel and Gavan Duffy wrote in an exaggerated way about the famine and that it was quite absurd for P. A. Sillard, the biographer of John Mitchel, to compare a respectable whig administrator, like Lord Clarendon, with the stern Elizabethan Lord Mountjoy, who destroyed the very crops of his enemies. These accusations may be exaggerated, but their influence on Irish thought and the sincerity with which they were made can hardly be doubted.

In the existing commentaries on the famine period, it is possible to detect two trends of thought related but yet distinct. On the one hand, we find that the more actively the writer was interested in political nationalism, the more determined he appeared to place full responsibility on the British government and its agents for what happened in Ireland. So it was with Gavan Duffy and later with Arthur Griffith, who could say that the British government deliberately used "the pretext of the failure of the potato crop to reduce the Celtic population by famine and exile." In contrast to this approach, we find the heirs of Fintan Lalor less willing to see in the Great Famine a conscious conspiracy against the nation. For them the disaster has a more organic, less deliberate origin. It was the social system rather than government which was at fault. James Connolly, in his acute analysis of Irish society, could declare: "No man who accepts capitalist society and the laws thereof can logically find fault with the statesmen of England for

their acts in that awful period."
But whether Connolly's important
reservations be accepted or not, the
famine, as a social phenomenon,
as a testing time for the 19th-century
state is entitled to the closest study
by the modern historian. The political
commentator, the ballad singer and
the unknown maker of folk-tales
have all spoken about the Great
Famine, but is there more to
be said?…

The traditional interpretation of the
Great Famine is fundamental to an
understanding of the character of Irish
society in the second half of the
19th century and later. But if modern
research cannot substantiate the
traditional in all its forms, something
surely more sobering emerges which is,
perhaps, of greater value towards an
appreciation of the problems that beset
all mankind, both the governors and
the governed in every generation. If
man, the prisoner of time, acts in
conformity with the conventions of
society into which he is born, it is
difficult to judge him with an
irrevocable harshness. So it is with
the men of the famine era. Human
limitations and timidity dominate
the story of the Great Famine, but of
great and deliberately imposed evil in
high positions of responsibility there is
little evidence. The really great evil
lay in the totality of that social
order which made such a famine
possible and which could tolerate,
to the extent it did, the sufferings
and hardship caused by the failure of
the potato crop.

Edited by R. Dudley Edwards and
T. Desmond Williams
*The Great Famine: Studies
in Irish History, 1845–52*
1956

*Revisionism revised: Cormac Ó Gráda on
Famine historiography.*

The historiography of the Great Famine
is curious. For a catastrophe usually
rated the key event in 19th-century Irish
history, it has produced remarkably
little serious academic research in
Ireland itself.…

What work there is takes some pains
to debunk the accounts of the "political
commentator, the ballad singer and
unknown maker of folk-tales." So too,
apparently, does the orthodoxy of the
third level classroom. Traditionalist
appraisals that even hint at culprits and
villains from across the Irish Sea tend
to get short shrift. From this anti-
populist perspective the current
orthodoxy is doubly reassuring. On
the one hand, far from being another
simple case of race murder, the Famine
is held to have been exaggerated in the
past by "emotive" nationalist propa-
gandists like John Mitchel and
O'Donovan Rossa, in terms of both
regional incidence and excess mortality.
On the other, what deaths there
were tend to be regarded as the largely
inevitable or unavoidable consequence
of economic backwardness.

Shattering dangerous myths about
the past is the historian's social
responsibility. In Ireland, where popular
history is an odd brew of myth and
reality, there is plenty for him to do.
Perhaps a dose of cold revisionism
was necessary to purge the locals
of a simplistic and hysterical…view of
the Famine as a "British plot"? The
connection between popular history and
nationalist resistance is, after all, real. It
was the IRA leader Ernie O'Malley who
wrote of the 1916 rising: "In the evening
I was in a whirl; my mind jumped
from a snatch of song to a remembered

page of economic history." Correcting nationalist misconceptions about historical grievances has been the unifying theme of revisionist Irish economic history for the last few decades. But when it comes to the Famine have Irish historians not allowed their "generosity and restraint" to run away with them? On the evidence, there is at least an argument to be put forward. Students of other famines seeking comparative insights may be impressed by the lack of Irish emotion or outrage, but they will quickly note too that themes central to mainstream famine history research have been ignored in Irish work....

A good example of the "generosity and restraint" view is the famous collection of essays *The Great Famine: Studies in Irish History,* edited in 1956 by the Dublin historians Dudley Edwards and Desmond Williams. Eschewing a narrative approach, the editors emphasized instead the Famine's roots deep in history, pointing to "the scale of the actual outlay to meet the famine," and in essence making excuses for the attitudes of British bureaucrats and politicians.... As a scholarly introduction to the Great Famine the Edwards and Williams volume lacks coherence and fairness.

What of the competition? By not attempting a general history Edwards and Williams in effect left it to the "popular" historian Cecil Woodham-Smith to fill the void a few years later. Woodham-Smith's enduring best-seller has its faults: it errs on several details, its understanding of the economic context is weak, and its interpretation of motives and events is sometimes cavalier. Still, looking back, it certainly deserved better than the chilly and delayed welcome accorded by the late

F. S. L. Lyons...[who] derided *The Great Hunger* for its naive populism and lack of humility. It was wrong of Woodham-Smith, he claimed, to criticize government outside its contemporary context; horrific descriptive accounts of the tragedy were all very well, but one must turn elsewhere for "the reason why." Students were asked to join in the fun of debunking Woodham-Smith; those taking an honours history degree at University College, Dublin, in 1963 were invited to write an essay on "*The Great Hunger* is a great novel." Orthodoxy has hardly changed since.... Robert Kee's graphic and "emotive" television history of 1980 met a worse fate than Woodham-Smith: it was heavily criticised by a leading Dublin academic for lending succour to terrorism....

Why have Irish historians shunned famine research? Why are outside historians less hidebound in their assessments? Politics is at least part of the answer; Irish historians are, by and large, a conservative bunch. There are no Irish E. P. Thompsons or Eugene Genoveses. But the considerable rhetorical challenge posed by "emotive" traditional accounts must also be a deterrent. Attempts at balance always risk being interpreted as making excuses. The Famine remains a sensitive subject, and perhaps that is why its economic and social history has not been written....

The current orthodoxy...tends to view the Great Famine as both unavoidable and inevitable. I see it instead as the tragic outcome of three factors: an ecological accident that could not have been predicted, and ideology ill geared to saving lives and, of course, mass poverty. The role of sheer bad luck is important: Ireland's ability to cope with a potato failure would have been far greater a few decades later, and the political will—and the political pressure—to spend more money to save lives greater too. If this post-revisionist interpretation of events of the 1840s comes closer to the traditional story, it also keeps its distance from the wilder populist interpretations mentioned earlier. Food availability *was* a problem; *nobody* wanted the extirpation of the Irish as a race.

Cormac Ó Gráda
Ireland Before and After the Famine: Explorations in Economic History, 1800–1925, 1988

The Famine and Ireland today: President Mary Robinson at Grosse Isle.

In this place of memory and regret I think we have a chance to reflect on our relation to the past [and to] the men and women who came here in the 1840s and died here helpless before an historical catastrophe of enormous proportions. It is their very helplessness which can mislead us into believing that we also are helpless in our attitude to a past we cannot control and can never change. But we are not. We have the chance to choose today between being spectators or participants at the vast theatre of human suffering which unfolds throughout human history.

If we are spectators then we will choose the view that there are inevitable historical victims and inevitable survivors. And from that view I believe comes a distancing which is unacceptable and unmoral.

If we are participants then we realise there are no inevitable victims. We refuse the temptation to distance ourselves from the suffering around us —whether it comes through history

books or contemporary television images. And then, although we cannot turn the clock back and change the deaths that happened here, at least we do justice to the reality of the people who died here by taking the meaning of their suffering and connecting it to the present-day challenges to our compassion and involvement. If we are participants we engage with the past in terms of the present. If we are spectators then we close these people into a prison of statistics and memories, from which they can never escape to challenge our conscience and compassion....

[As] President of Ireland, and in memory of so many who died here, I think I can say that what is particularly Irish about this occasion is not simply the nationality of those who died here. It is also our sense, as a people who suffered and survived, that our history does not entitle us to a merely private catalogue of memories. Instead it challenges us to consider, not just little Ellen Keane, the four-year-old child who was the first person to die here in 1847, but the reality that children are usually the first victims of famine and displacement. It challenges us, in her name, to consider with compassion and anger those other children to whom we can give no name who are dying today in Rwanda and whom I saw in the camps in Somalia.

Next year commemorates the 150th year since the famine which devastated Ireland. No one then could have foreseen, or even hoped, that a modern European state would emerge, with a powerful identity and a confident culture. It is very important to me that within that culture the voiceless, desolate dead of such places as Grosse Ile are remembered and honoured. We owe to their humiliation at the hands of fate just as much love and respect as to any brave or decisive action which turned the tide of history in our favour. But it is also important that as a people who have seen the dark and the bright face of such fortunes we take the initiative not just in compassionate action towards those who are now caught, as we once were, in famine and disease, but also in re-defining the contemporary attitude to such suffering.

We are in the presence, even as I speak, of an enormous historic irony. The ease and proliferation of communication has had, I believe, the result of isolating us further from one another. The presence of death in our living rooms, the images of horror invite us to feel helpless and fatalistic. Perhaps the real justice we can do these people here and those who died throughout our famine—perhaps the best way to commemorate them—is to think decisively and creatively about the supply and distribution of such ordinary commodities as food and water....

Grosse Ile is not simply a place to commemorate the past and honour those who are buried here. In essence, it is a resource to connect us with the terrible realities of our current world. It challenges us to reject the concept of inevitable victims, and, having done so, to face up to the consequences of that rejection.

Address by the President of Ireland,
Mary Robinson,
at Grosse Isle, Canada,
21 August 1994

Mary Robinson, President of Ireland, greets Irish Canadians at Grosse Isle, August 1994.

IRELAND
in 1848

Further Reading

Akenson, Donald Harman, *The Irish Diaspora: A Primer*, P. D. Meany Co., Toronto, 1993

Bourke, Austin, *"The Visitation of God?" The Potato and the Great Irish Famine*, Lilliput Press, Dublin, 1993

Boyce, D. George, *Nationalism in Ireland*, 2nd ed., Routledge, London, 1991

Coleman, Terry, *Passage to America*, Pimlico Press, London, 1972

Crawford, E. Margaret, ed., *Famine: The Irish Experience 900–1900. Subsistence Crises and Famines in Ireland*, John Donald Publishers, Edinburgh, 1989

Cullen, L. M., *An Economic History of Ireland since 1660*, 2nd ed., B. T. Batsford, London, 1987

Daly, Mary E., *The Famine in Ireland*, Dundalgan Dublin Historical Assoc., Dundalk, 1986

Edwards, R. D., and T. D. Williams, eds., *The Great*

Famine: Studies in Irish History, 1845–52, 1956. New ed., with introduction by Cormac Ó Gráda, Lilliput Press, Dublin, 1994

Fitzpatrick, David, *Irish Emigration 1801–1921*, Economic and Social History of Ireland, Dublin, 1984

Foster, R. F., *Modern Ireland 1600–1972*, Viking Penguin, New York, 1988

Hoppen, K. Theodore, *Ireland since 1800: Conflict and Conformity*, Longmans, Harlow, 1989

Kerr, Donal A., *"A Nation of Beggars?": Priests, People and Politics in Famine Ireland 1846–1852*, Clarendon Press, Oxford, 1994

Kinealy, Christine, *This Great Calamity: The Irish Famine 1845–52*, Gill and Macmillan, Dublin, 1994

MacKay, Donald, *Flight from Famine: The Coming of the Irish to Canada*, McClelland and Stewart, Toronto, 1990

Miller, Kerby A., *Emigrants and Exiles:*

Ireland and the Irish Exodus to North America, Oxford University Press, New York, 1985

————, and Paul Wagner, *Out of Ireland: The Story of Irish Emigration to America*, Elliott and Clark, Washington, D.C., 1994

Mokyr, Joel, *Why Ireland Starved: A Quantitative and Analytical History of the Irish Economy, 1800–1850*, Routledge, Chapman, and Hall, New York 1983

Nowlan, Kevin B., *The Politics of Repeal: A Study in the Relations between Great Britain and Ireland, 1841–50*, Routledge and Kegan Paul, London, 1965

O'Farrell, Patrick, *The Irish in Australia*, revised ed., New South Wales University Press, Kensington, New South Wales, 1993

Ó Gráda, Cormac, *The Great Irish Famine*, Macmillan, New York, 1989

————, *Ireland Before and After the Famine: Explorations in Economic History, 1800–1925*,

Manchester University Press, Manchester, 1988

————, *Ireland: A New Economic History 1780–1939*, Oxford University Press, New York, 1994

Ó Tuathaigh, Gearóid, *Ireland Before the Famine 1798–1848*, Gill and Macmillan, Dublin, 1972

Póirtéir, Cathal, ed., *The Great Irish Famine*, Mercier Press, Cork, 1995

Scally, Robert James, *The End of Hidden Ireland: Rebellion, Famine and Emigration*, Oxford University Press, New York, 1995

Swift, Roger, and Sheridan Gilley, eds., *The Irish in Britain 1815–1939*, Pinter Publishers, London, 1989

Vaughan, W. E., ed., *A New History of Ireland, Vol. V: Ireland under the Union, I, 1801–70*, Oxford University Press, New York, 1989

Woodham-Smith, Cecil, *The Great Hunger: Ireland 1845–1849*, Hamish Hamilton, London, 1962

List of Illustrations

Key: *a*=above; *b*=below; *c*=center; *l*=left; *r*=right
Abbreviations:
CMAG=Crawford Municipal Art Gallery, Cork; UCD=Department of Folklore, University College Dublin; GL= Guildhall Library,

London; *ILN=The Illustrated London News*; LC=Library of Congress, Washington, D.C.; NGI=National Gallery of Ireland, Dublin; NLI=National Library of Ireland, Dublin; UFTM=Ulster Folk and

Transport Museum

Front cover Detail, *The Discovery of the Potato Blight in Ireland*. Painting by Daniel McDonald, c. 1847. UCD. Detail, Potato plant. Watercolor by Claude and Denise Millet

Spine and back cover
Detail, Potato plant. Watercolor by Claude and Denise Millet

1 The Discovery of the Potato Blight in Ireland. Painting by Daniel McDonald, c. 1847. UCD

2 Irish Emigrants Waiting

Index

Acknowledgments

The author and publishers wish to thank Kevin Whelan, Janice Holmes, and Sara Jan for reading and commenting on the text. Thanks are also due to Luke Dodd of the Famine Museum, Strokestown, the Gorry Gallery, Dublin, John Joe Kilcoyne of the Famine Centre, Louisburgh, Elizabeth Kirwan of the National Library of Ireland, and Don Mullan of Concern, for advice and assistance.

Photo Credits

Atlas van Stolk, Rotterdam 14b; Belfast Harbour Commissioners 59a; Birmingham Museum and Art Gallery 67b; Jacques Boissinot/Canadian Press 183; Bridgeman Art Library/Giraudon 17b, 104–5; British Library, London 15, 129; British Museum, London 42a, 43b, 86a, 127; Calderdale Museums, Halifax 64a; Christie's, New York 119; The Company of Merchant Adventurers of the City of York 38b; Crawford Municipal Art Gallery, Cork 8–9, 36, 50b; Department of Folklore, University College Dublin front cover, 1, 27, 30, 62, 98; Dundee Art Galleries and Museums 117; E. T. Archive 11; Famine Museum, Strokestown 25b, 46, 58b, 126–7, 172; Giraudon 43a, 76; The Gorry Gallery, Dublin 3, 32a, 122; Guildhall Library, London 17a, 31, 33, 34, 35a, 38a, 45, 46–7, 51b, 132, 144, 160; Irish Architectural Archive, Dublin 28–9a; Johannesburg Art Gallery 110–1; Keystone 115b; Leeds City Art Gallery 18a; Leicester Museum and Art Gallery 70–1; Library of Congress, Washington, D. C. 108a, 109b, 112b, 115a, 151; Museum of the City of New York 6–7; Museum of the City of New York, The J. Clarence Davies Collection 114; National Archives, Dublin 41; National Galleries of Scotland, Edinburgh 103; National Gallery of Ireland, Dublin 4–5, 14a, 20a, 23a, 72–3, 75a; National Library of Ireland, Dublin 12, 18b, 24a, 40b, 56, 57, 58a, 59b, 60, 66a, 66b, 84b, 95, 96, 97, 162; National Portrait Gallery, London 40a; New-York Historical Society 112a; The Oakland Museum History Department, A. J. Russell Collection 113; Daphne Pochin-Mould 28–9 inset; The Royal Collection. © Her Majesty the Queen 90–1, 92–3a; St John's Seminary, Brighton, Massachusetts 55a; Science Museum, London 116; Sheffield Art Museums 2, 23b, 69; The Slide File, Dublin 128; Sotheby's Transparency Library, London 36b, 37; Ulster Folk and Transport Museum 16, 24b, 32b, 42b, 120, 130, 176; Ulster Museum, Belfast 99a, 118–9; Watts Gallery, Compton, Guildford 80, 81; Whitworth Art Gallery, University of Manchester 26; Williamson Art Gallery and Museum, Birkenhead 13.

Text Credits

Grateful acknowledgment is made for use of material from the following works: (pp. 133–6) *Alexis de Tocqueville's Journey in Ireland: July–August, 1835*, translated and edited by Emmet Larkin, Catholic University of America Press; reprinted by permission of Catholic University of America Press, Washington, D.C. (pp. 176–7) Eavan Boland, "That the Science of Cartography is Limited," *In a Time of Violence*, 1994; reprinted from *In a Time of Violence* by Eavan Boland with the permission of W. W. Norton & Company, Inc. Copyright © 1994 by Eavan Boland. (pp. 163–4) Máire Ní Dhroma, "Amhrán na bPrátaí Dubha," translated by Cormac Ó Gráda as "The Song of the Black Potatoes"; reprinted by permission of Cormac Ó Gráda. (pp. 179–80) *The Great Famine: Studies in Irish History 1845–1852*, edited by R. Dudley Edwards and T. Desmond Williams, 1956; reprinted by kind permission of The Educational Company of Ireland, Dublin. (pp. 174–5) Seamus Heaney, "At a Potato Digging," *Death of a Naturalist*, Faber and Faber, 1966; reprinted by permission of Faber and Faber Ltd. (pp. 175–6) John Hewitt, "The Scar," *The Collected Poems of John Hewitt*, edited by Frank Ormsby, Blackstaff Press, 1991; reprinted by permission of Blackstaff Press, Dundonald, Belfast. (pp. 173–4) Donagh Macdonagh, "The Hungry Grass"; reprinted by permission of Faber and Faber Ltd. (pp. 172–3) Liam O'Flaherty, *Famine*, 1937; reprinted by permission of Wolfhound Press, Dublin. (pp. 180–2) Cormac Ó Gráda, *Ireland Before and After the Famine: Explorations in Economic History, 1800–1925*, Manchester University Press, 1988; reprinted by permission of Manchester University Press, Manchester.

Peter Gray was born in Belfast in 1965 and
was educated there and at Cambridge University.
After completing a doctoral thesis on the politics
of the Irish Famine, he taught British and
Irish history at Queen's University, Belfast, and
Birkbeck College, London, before being appointed
to a British Academy Postdoctoral Fellowship at
Downing College, Cambridge, in 1993.
He is a member of the editorial board
of the journal *History Ireland*.

To my parents

For Harry N. Abrams, Inc.
Editor: Sarah Burns
Typographic Designer: Elissa Ichiyasu
Design Supervisor: Miko McGinty
Assistant Designer: Tina Thompson

Library of Congress Catalog Card Number: 95-75658

ISBN 0-8109-2895-7